MAPLE LEAF ROUTE : CAEN

Terry Copp and Robert Vogel

ISBN 0 919907-01-6

Designed and Typeset by
Stephen Graphic Services.
Film by St. Jacobs Printery.
Printed by The Beacon Herald Fine Printing Division

Published by Maple Leaf Route,
Alma, Ontario N0B 1A0.

Contents

Why? 1

German Strategy 1944 8

Operation Overlord 14

The Canadians 20

Operation Neptune 26

The 8th Brigade Landings 38

The 7th Brigade Landings 48

Advance Inland D-Day 56

The German Reaction 62

The 9th Brigade Advance 68

Attack on the 7th Brigade 74

Allied Strategy 84

German Strategy 90

Carpiquet 98

Caen 106

Retrospect 118

This volume is dedicated to the men of the 3rd Canadian Infantry Division.

FOREWORD

MAPLE LEAF ROUTE: CAEN is the first volume in a new series on the Canadian campaign in Northwest Europe, 1944-1945. This volume contains the story of the planning of Overlord and the details of Canadian operations during the first month of the campaign.

The authors have gone back to the primary sources to present a fresh account of the strategy and tactics of both the Allied and German Armies. The text is complimented by contemporary photographs, War Art, a new series of maps oriented to illustrate the thrust of the Allied assault, and facsimiles of War Diaries from Canadian Infantry regiments.

The title of the series comes from the symbol used to mark the path that Canadians travelled on their long road to victory - the Maple Leaf Route.

Why?

The sector of the Normandy coast code-named 'Juno' gradually came into view - five miles of coastline which at low tide was bounded by wide sandy beaches. The maps, air photos and wave-top pictures had familiarized the officers with the landmarks. There, on the extreme right, were the lighthouse and wireless mast that marked the junction between 'Juno' and 'Gold', the area to be attacked by the British 50th Division. In the centre, two and one-half miles along a low shoreline, was the small port of Courseulles-sur-Mer at the mouth of the River Seulles which separated 'Mike' and 'Nan' beaches. A short distance east, high church steeples identified the two seaside villages, Bernières and St. Aubin. Immediately behind the coastline the countryside was open, rising very gradually towards Carpiquet the divisional objective.

It was time to go. The assault on Hitler's Atlantic Wall, was about to begin. The young men of Canada's 3rd Infantry Division, drawn from all parts of the country, were set to do battle for the liberation of western Europe. Some were to die that day and many to be wounded. In the weeks and months that followed the casualty lists would grow, men would be killed, maimed and driven beyond the edge of human endurance. Why were they there?

The Second World War engulfed the world in violence on an unprecedented scale. There has never been another conflict which has involved so many different parts of the world or brought so much suffering and death. The people who went to war against Hitler's Germany believed that they were involved in a crusade to destroy a force of such great evil that there was no other solution than total victory, no other strategy but total war. In the end the Allies were triumphant, but many people came to believe that the war, which had been fought to defeat a specific challenge to humanity, should somehow have rid the world of all forms of violence and evil. Instead the postwar world seemed full of conflict, repression and inhumanity. What then was the point of the enormous sacrifices by civilians and soldiers alike? Had it all been in vain?

In 1939 the people of the Allied Nations went to war with a sense of indignation and resignation, not with any sense of adventure or quest for glory. It was a decision taken reluctantly and with a feeling of horror but a decision which most people felt was necessary. The events of the previous decade seemed to have made it so.

After the First World War, the people of the countries which had fought in it, as well as those who had only watched the slaughter on the battlefields of Europe, seemed determined never again to fight a major war. Even the people of the victorious powers were so emotionally and economically exhausted that they rapidly lost interest in the fruits of their victory and rejected attempts to glorify the war.

This was the view of the majority but some believed that even greater violence was necessary to attain their political ends. So there grew up a few political ideologies which sought authoritarian order and conquest. In the climate of the 1920's it was hard to take such ideas seriously. Perhaps because so many had experienced or witnessed the reality of the battlefield, they were not prepared to oppose by force the imposition of these ideologies even upon themselves. That occurred in a few countries but it was not until the end of the decade that the inability of existing institutions to overcome the accumulating crises, gave credence to advocates of outrageous solutions.

Nowhere was this more evident than in the Germany which fell under the control of Hitler in 1933. It is true that between 1933 and 1939, he promised more violence than actually occurred but he had, before the outbreak of war, nevertheless destroyed or neutralized all the institutions in Germany which might have curbed his ambition and power. In Hitler's political view, the German Revolution of 1918 had interrupted an otherwise successful war. Once he had created conditions within Germany which would make the repetition of such a revolution impossible, and the destruction of the German institutions was that condition, then he would continue the interrupted war on his own terms. In his eyes the Peace Treaty of 1919 was the international manifestation of the results of the betrayal of the German people by the Weimar Republic. The Treaty would have been unjust to a defeated Germany, but

"D-Day" by Charles Wood (10558).

3

it was doubly humiliating because he did not believe that Germany had really been defeated by her external enemies.

Therefore, his first aim in foreign policy was to abolish the Treaty of Versailles. Of course by the time he came to power, the most troublesome economic burdens imposed by the Treaty had already been abandoned. That left the military restrictions and any possible adjustment to Germany's boundaries. Between 1933 and the remilitarization of the Rhineland in 1936, Hitler succeeded in freeing Germany from the military limitations imposed by the Treaty, a relatively easy policy in view of the fact that the other states generally had shown themselves ready to accept major adjustments in the power configuration of Europe. From then on, the crises in Europe mounted and the intervals between grew shorter as Hitler correctly estimated the reluctance of the other states to engage in another war. The crises in 1938 and 1939 followed each other with breathtaking rapidity and in each he scored yet another triumph. But his triumphs were won only because his adversaries (they were not yet his enemies) misunderstood his ultimate goals.

They believed him to be placing Germany in a position commensurate with her size and her economic capacity. Indeed if his ambition had been to reassert the pre-eminent place of Germany in Europe, then the outcome of the Munich crisis should have brought 'Peace in our Time'. But that was not his aim and therefore he was never, as has sometimes been maintained, just another German statesman. The occupation of Prague in March 1939 revealed that, and his adversaries began to understand that they were dealing with a man who not only said that he believed that all history was a bloody struggle of 'races' but who would act as though that were the truth. Many had previously felt revulsion for his domestic policies, the violence of his language, his systematic harrassment of the Jews, his ruthless exploitation of the weak, but the statesmen of Europe had been reluctant to act in a manner which would make war inevitable and plunge the world into a conflict made more terrible by the advent of weapons, like the bomber, which threatened the destruction not only of men in the armies, but of women and children in the cities.

Of course these statesmen were suspicious of each other, of course each preferred that another take the first step and of course, each wanted to avoid bringing the horrors, which they knew would follow, on the heads of their own citizens. But fundamentally they could not believe, before 1939, that there was not a way to find a settlement with Hitler. No effective alliance could be created in the last year of peace because the major powers had been too divided by the very fact of each one trying to find a settlement least harmful to its own interests. Hitler's greatest asset was always the ability to sense the weakness of his opponents and their reluctance to enter into a war for which they were neither spiritually nor militarily prepared. That gave him the opportunity to consolidate his position in central Europe and to achieve two years of continuous victories after the outbreak of war.

Canadians, like everyone else, went to war with few illusions, certainly not with the illusion of going to help the British Empire for the sake of Imperial unity. They had followed with considerable sophistication the events in Europe over the last few years. There was considerable understanding of the evil which Hitler represented and horror at the thought of the continuing expansion of his domain. Canada would not have gone to war if Britain had failed to live up to her Polish guarantee. However, there is no doubt about the realistic attitude of the majority of Canadians who saw the war not in the sense of Britain's enemy being Canada's enemy, but rather in the sense that what Hitler represented was truly the enemy of all that in which Canadians believed. As the war progressed and the horrors of Hitler's New Order became more evident there was little to make Canadians feel that they had made the wrong decision.

Wars are fought to make peace. The Allied powers in the Second World War fought to make peace, even if they all had somewhat different views about what the peace should bring. But in this they were in marked contrast to Hitler, who had no ideas about peace since he believed that the history of the world was an endless racial struggle for domination. The people of 1939-45 understood, perhaps better than the present generation does, that despite the existence of evil, both in themselves and

Nuremberg Rally,
1937

in others, it is sometimes necessary to deal with the greater evil before one can hope to cope with the lesser ones.

It was with this understanding that the soldiers and the civilians suffered and died. If we cannot acknowledge with pride that with their achievements and sacrifices they destroyed an enormous wrong, we are in danger of becoming contemptuous of that generation which contributed so much to make the postwar period, with all its problems, infinitely more humane than it would have been had Hitler's ideas triumphed in this world.

'You ask what is our policy? I will say: It is to wage war, by sea, land, and air, with all our might and with all the strength that God can give us: to wage war against a monstrous tyranny, never surpassed in the dark, lamentable catalogue of human crime. That is our policy. You ask what is our aim? I can answer in one word: Victory — victory at all costs, victory in spite of all terror; victory, however hard and long the road may be; for without victory, there is no survival.'

Winston Churchill, May 13, 1940

Adolf Hitler at Nuremberg, 1937.

German Strategy-1944

"In 1918 we lost the war because of a 'Fleet in being',
we will lose the present one because of an 'Army in being!'"

So thought the officers of the German army fighting for its existence in Russia in the Spring of 1944. They regarded the 'Army in being' in Western Europe as the reason for this inability to obtain adequate reinforcements from the German High Command (OKW). In a hard-hitting report which was distributed down to divisional level, they claimed that while 53% of the army was fighting for the survival of the German people, 47% was standing idly by.

A somewhat apologetic reply from OKW pointed out that in fact there were only 41 divisions capable of fighting on the Eastern Front in all the other military areas controlled by OKW and that 20 of those were in fact in combat zones. It went on to say that 23 divisions and a number of assault-gun companies had been sent to the east since July 1943 and that the divisions of the C. in C. West (OB.West) had recently given 45,000 fit young soldiers to the Eastern Front. Moreover, any withdrawal in Italy or in south-eastern Europe (The Balkans), would increase rather than decrease the frontage that needed to be defended. In fact, there were only 21 divisions of any value behind the coastlines threatened by an invasion.

Despite this response to the complaints from the Eastern Front, OKW had in fact accomplished a great deal in building up the German defences in the West since the Hitler Directive No. 51 of November 3rd, 1943. The directive itself is interesting in that it recognizes that, in previous years, the main exertions of the army had been in the east and acknowledges that the vast extent of the conquered territory 'makes it possible for us to lose ground, even on a large scale, without a fatal blow being dealt to the nervous system of Germany. No such option exists in the West and, therefore, the Western forces must be built up to withstand a landing and, if a landing succeeds, to launch a decisive counter-attack'.

The directive spelled out specifically the equipment to be sent to the West and demanded that 'careful and detailed emergency plans must be drawn up so that everything we have in Germany and in the coastal areas not attached, and which is in any way capable of action, is hurled immediately against the invading enemy'. The Airforce, the Navy and the Waffen SS were included, the airforce being ordered to prepare emergency airfields and 'ruthlessly strip' even the Home Defence fighter force in order to meet the invader. Commanders-in-Chief were ordered to cooperate and report their dispositions and plans by November 15th.

Although the Eastern Front continued to obtain some reinforcements through the winter and spring of 1943-44, a substantial build up of materials did take place in the West. In February 1943 there were 32 divisions in the West. In the course of the year, 33 divisions were moved out while 39 were added, the majority of which were new divisions - that is, divisions activated from reserves. At the end of the year there were, therefore, 38 divisions available in the West. Between January and May 1944 the position changed more rapidly in favour of OB. West; 23 divisions were added and only 7 dispatched, so that by May 31st there were 54 divisions available for the defence of France and the Low Countries.

Equally important was the build-up of tracked armoured vehicles during the same period. On the 31st December, 1943, OB West had 879 such vehicles, but on 31st May, 1944 there were 1,622 of which 514 were Panther tanks and 101 Tiger tanks. The Fuehrer directive had had its effects on the strength of the Western defences at least as far as ground forces were concerned.

The improvement in the situation needs to be seen in the perspective of the general increase in German production and the high state of mobilization of its manpower resources, which occurred in the first six months of 1944. For instance, the total armoured vehicle establishment of the German forces rose, despite heavy losses, from 7,233 on 1st January, 1944 to 10,484 on 1st June, 1944. OB West, therefore, had only 15% of the available vehicles. Similarly in terms of manpower, while there is difficulty in establishing the exact ratio between various fronts because of the variety of units involved, the troops available to OB. West represented only between 15% to 19% of the combat forces of the Third Reich.

Field Marshall Erwin Rommel inspecting the Atlantic Wall

Moreover, there were important differences of quality among the 54 divisions available to OB. West. Of the 36 infantry divisions stationed there, 23 were static defence units which, unable to move, were frozen into defensive positions along the coast. The 3 field divisions of the Luftwaffe were the result of the poor compromise between the refusal of the Luftwaffe to give up its excess manpower and the army's need for soldiers. The 3 parachute divisions of the Luftwaffe were generally better trained and equipped and were full of enthusiastic volunteers. A security division was largely tied to policing Paris and there were a number of reserve units not counted into the total of 54 divisions.

The main striking force was, of course, the armoured contingent of the Command. There were 9 armoured divisions stationed in the West in various stages of completing training or refitting and there was one Panzer Grenadier (Mobile) division, the 17th SS. Altogether there were 4 SS divisions amongst the armoured forces, usually more lavishly equipped and manned than the equivalent units in the army, but even among these, there were substantial variations. The 12th SS had an almost full establishment of tanks (150), as well as 20,540 men. The 17th SS Panzer Grenadier, on the other hand, which mustered 17,321 men on June 1st, had only 37 assault guns and no tanks. The Fuehrer directive 51, which had called for at least 93 Mark IV tanks for all Panzer and Panzer Grenadier divisions, had only been partially fulfilled.

The weakest part of the German defence structure was the inability of the High Command to agree on a coherent strategy. Plans were drawn up and abandoned. The possibility that the Allies would land at several widely divergent places at different times seemed to make hazardous the movement of troops from their defensive positions. By March 1944 OKW gave up the idea of having a prepared plan for concentrating troops from the apparently non-threatened areas in order to prepare a counter-attack.

Indeed, the German High Command remained bitterly divided about the best way of opposing the Allied landing. The basic question was whether to put the bulk of the available resources into defending the beaches, or to hold on to a strong central reserve which could deliver a counter-attack once the enemy's intentions were clear. This same dilemma had faced the British High Command in 1940-41 as they contemplated the invasion of England and had led to serious differences of opinion between Alanbrooke and Montgomery, on one side, advocating a mobile defence, and Ironside and Auchinleck, on the other side, proposing that the beaches be defended to the utmost. 'I am sure', wrote Auchinleck, 'that we should make every effort to prevent the enemy from landing on the beach. I still believe that this is his most difficult task ...'. Rommel, in 1944, was of the same opinion.

The Germans of course, had more time to build up their defences, but whereas the British could expect to make considerable improvements every month in their manpower and equipment, the German situation, while improving, was always subject to sudden calls for men and material from the Russian or the Italian fronts. Moreover, the situation of the German airforce was steadily deteriorating and the German surface fleet had never been capable of seriously challenging British superiority in the Channel.

Beginning in 1942, the German High Command had begun to fortify the major ports, considering correctly that the Allies would need to capture some major ports in order to sustain a large force in Europe. They then went on to build a series of fortifications along the most vulnerable stretches of coastline. Due to the continuous shortage of manpower, these fortifications were manned by 'static' divisions, units that had no transport facilities or reconnaisance companies and relatively few heavy weapons (other than those dug in) to defend the beaches. The divisions were, therefore, fixed in their coastal sectors and could only be moved if transport was provided and the dug-in equipment largely abandonned. Then, of course, they would hardly be useful fighting units, especially since their lack of mobility tempted the German High Command to strip these divisions of their younger men, because physical fitness was not a high priority for static defence.

The divisions became smaller in manpower, partly in conformity with

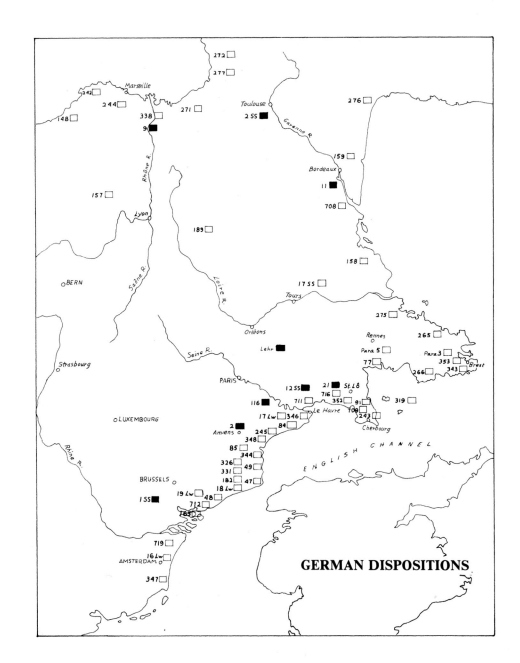

GERMAN DISPOSITIONS

the general reorganization and reduction in the size of infantry divisions in 1943 and again in 1944, but they rarely received the new weapons to compensate for the reduction in manpower that the reorganization had envisioned. Even the main manpower losses were often made up by East European conscripts or volunteers (Ost battalions) which had little fighting value. The possibility of up-grading even some of these divisions to give flexibility to the defence seemed out of the question in 1944, although attempts were made to create mobile (bicycle mounted) combat groups. The 'Atlantic Wall' mentality had seriously limited the options available to OB West.

Field-Marshall Rundstedt had been appointed Commander of Army Group D, renamed C. in C. West, in March 1942 and Hitler had issued a comprehensive directive (No. 40) for the defence of the West. Even this attempt to rationalize the command structure had failed to give OB West adequate control of naval and airforces, although the directive might have been interpreted to do so. In any case, Rundstedt had too few forces at his disposal to oppose any serious landing other than raids such as the Dieppe assault of August 1942. His constant complaints about the inadequacy of his troops, both in quantity and quality, finally elicited the Hitler Directive No. 51 but it also brought him a difficult partner in the shape of Field-Marshall Rommel.

After the defeat of his Africa Corps, Rommel had been made commander of Army Group B, a Headquarters for Special Employment, used during the autumn in Northern Italy to 'pacify' that area in case of an Italian 'betrayal'. Rommel fulfilled this mission but he did not get the Supreme Command which went to Kesselring on October 25th, 1943. Rommel and his Army Group HQ went home to Munich, but he was quickly reassigned as Inspector of Fortifications for the whole of the coastline from Denmark to the Italian border to report directly to Hitler on the state of the fortifications. Army Group B was soon moved to France, at first ostensibly to take over control of an invasion front but, in fact, as an operational headquarters interposed between OB. West and the 7th and 15th Armies, the two armies lying along that coastline which was the most likely scene of the Allied invasion. Before the invasion,

German Gun position on the Atlantic Wall. DND PMR 82-079

Rundstedt had been successful in creating a more orderly structure by setting up a second army group, Army Group G. which controlled the Biscay coast (1st Army) and the Mediterranean coastline of France (19th Army). Nevertheless, despite Rundstedt's attempt to have two subordinate army groups, leaving him with the overall direction of the campaign, Rommel's influence on the OKW staff and with Hitler remained very powerful.

Rommel believed that his experience in Africa had taught him that armoured divisions were incapable of proper movement in the face of Allied air superiority. He was convinced, therefore, that the Allied landings had to be defeated on the beaches and that to this end all available German troops had to be stationed as close to the coastline as possible. He objected even to having a second line of defence, a line which Rundstedt had laboriously built up along the Channel coast. Rommel prevented the building of such a line in Normandy.

While his headquarters became operational on January 1st, 1944, Rommel threw himself with characteristic energy into the job of making the beaches impregnable. He had been chosen for the position in part because his reputation was likely to convince the troops in the area of the importance of their task. He travelled indefatigably up and down the French coast, exhorting men to build obstacles on the beaches, inventing devices which would damage or sink landing craft, planting stakes on flat fields to prevent gliders from landing. He obtained large quantities of captured French ammunition in order to fasten explosives to his obstacles and he advocated the laying of huge minefields off the coast. He assumed that the Allies would land at high tide and so placed most of the obstacles high on the beach. The Allies did not oblige. Finally he wanted to obtain control of the armoured divisions in order to place them close enough to the front so that they could intervene during the first actual landing of the enemy.

This last demand created a serious problem because Rundstedt believed that it would be necessary to fight a more mobile battle if the Allies succeeded in establishing a bridgehead in France. With this in mind, he had set up in November 1943, a headquarters (Panzer Group West) for training his mobile divisions. He felt that this training function was necessary because these divisions were either in the process of forming or had been returned from the east for rest and refitting. Rundstedt planned that 'Panzer Group West' would direct a properly coordinated counter-offensive when and if that became necessary. Geyr von Schweppenburg, the commander of Panzer Group West did not agree with Rommel's ideas about the role of the Panzer divisions, and the experience of the Anzio beachhead counter-offensive (January-February 1944) would seem to have supported his reservations by illustrating the difficulties of counter-attacking within the range of naval gunfire.

The whole matter was debated at a Fuehrer conference in March 1944. Rommel demanded an extension of his authority to include all of the mobile reserves and the 1st and 19th armies, in effect making him a second C. in C. West. Hitler at first agreed but OKW, in working out the details, partly reversed this decision. The result was an impossible compromise. Rommel obtained control over 3 Panzer divisions (2nd, 21st and 116th), Army Group G remained subordinate to Rundstedt but obtained control of three Panzer divisions also. (2nd SS, 9th and 11th), while OKW insisted on the final control over the movement of the remaining four (1st SS, 12th SS, 17th SS Panzer Grenadier and Panzer Div. Lehr). Rundstedt regarded this last point as a pure formality, but the total solution had created a situation in which no single headquarters had control over all the mobile reserves. Perhaps, even more detrimental for any kind of reasonable defence beyond the beaches, there was no infantry reserve at all. If the Allies managed to break through the fortified coastline, the only defence left was to commit the armoured divisions and Rommel's refusal to create a second line and his control of the three armoured divisions meant that they would be committed as quickly as possible. Any attempt on the part of 'Panzer Group West' to organize an effective counter-attack was vitiated by the fact that there were so few Panzer divisions left. In any event, Rommel had allowed himself no choice but to commit them piecemeal early in the battle.

The Atlantic Wall by O.N. Fisher (12416).

Operation Overlord

When Franklin Roosevelt and Winston Churchill left the Quebec Conference in August, 1943 the long and frequently bitter debate over the timing of a 'Second Front' in Northwest Europe was finally over. Since the Spring of 1942 the two allies had been at odds over the most fundamental questions of grand strategy. Churchill and the British Chiefs of Staff, fearing casualties similar to those experienced in the First World War, sought ways of weakening Germany before the major offensive was launched. They wanted to disperse German military power by attacking in the Mediterranean while the heavy bombers reduced German production and morale. With luck they might even avoid the necessity for an invasion of France.

US military leaders, on the other hand, were reluctant to wait and suspicious of what they saw as Britain's imperial interest in the Mediterranean. General Marshall in particular, was convinced that the only sound strategy was a direct attack on Germany by the shortest possible route. The debate was played out against the background of events in Russia. The British feared a repetition of the Russian collapse of 1917 and the prospect of the entire weight of the German Army being directed against the Allied Forces. The Americans replied that an early invasion of Europe was the best way to prevent a Russian defeat.

Churchill rejected the American plan to invade France in 1942 and won Roosevelt's support for 'Torch', the landings in French North Africa. US military leaders reacted to this decision by abandoning hope for a Second Front in 1943 and diverting US energies to the Pacific. Now at last at Quebec City a date (May 1944), a place (Normandy), and a plan had been agreed upon.

The plan had been drawn up by a staff working under the direction of Britain's Lt. General Frederick Morgan. He had been appointed Chief of Staff to the Supreme Allied Commander (COSSAC) in May 1943 but there was still no agreement on who that Supreme Commander should be. The planners had confronted a very difficult task. Though experience in assault landings had been gained at Dieppe, North Africa and Sicily, 'Neptune' the assault phase of 'Overlord', presented some very special

problems. Morgan was forced to work within guidelines which allowed for a three-division (plus airborne) initial attack. The key to success was, therefore, rapid landings of additional troops and supplies on the captured beachhead. There had to be enough shipping available to double the number of troops onshore in twenty-four hours and to bring the equivalent of twenty-one divisions to the battlefront in just twelve days.

The chosen area, the Calvodos coast of Normandy, contained only minor ports, so the planners had worked out an extraordinary scheme of creating two man-made harbours - 'Mulberries' - and a number of artificial breakwaters called 'Gooseberries'. Everyone agreed that the early capture of Cherbourg was vital to success but it was hoped that the prefabricated harbours would allow for continuous unloading of supplies into the beachhead while Cherbourg was captured and its port repaired.

Apart from the problem of supply COSSAC had established four criteria which had to be met if the landings were to be successful. (1) The enemy must remain ignorant of the proposed landing site; (2) he must be prevented from bringing up reinforcements quickly once the Allies had landed; (3) there must be complete Allied air and naval superiority in the English Channel; (4) the local defences must be largely destroyed by air and sea bombardment.

A series of deception plans were used to draw enemy attention to a variety of possible landing sites and eventually to persuade them that the main landings would take place in the Pas de Calais.

By January, 1944 the Supreme Commander, General Dwight D. Eisenhower and his own Chief of Staff, Walter Bedell Smith, had taken over direction of the Overlord Plan with General Morgan acting as Smith's deputy. Eisenhower had brought Air Marshall Arthur Tedder with him from the Mediterranean as his Deputy Commander and co-ordinator of the Allied air effort. Admiral Bertram Ramsay of the Royal Navy controlled the naval forces. For ground commander, Eisenhower had asked for General Harold Alexander, another member of

This photograph of the Allied Military leaders was taken on February 1, 1944. The camera has caught the commanders at a symbolic moment: Montgomery expounds, Eisenhower listens patiently, Bradley and Tedder react characteristically. (Left to right) Bradley, Tedder, Ramsay, Leigh-Mallory, Eisenhower, Bedell-Smith, Montgomery. PA 129050/Public Archives Canada

Eisenhower's successful team in the Mediterranean. Instead he got Bernard L. Montgomery, the victor of El Alamein and the most famous British general of the war.

Supreme Headquarters Allied Expeditionary Force (SHAEF) quickly got down to work on the details of the plan. A five division front was authorized and the methods of preventing the Germans from reinforcing the frontline were worked out with the various airforce commanders. The air plan called for the disruption of the French railway network and the destruction of rail and road bridges across the rivers Seine and Loire. It was strongly opposed by the 'Bomber Barons' Air Marshal Harris and Lt. General Doolittle, but the railway marshalling yards were struck with considerable precision, wreaking havoc with the French transportation system. No pattern to the raids could be determined by the Germans and they read the destruction of the Seine bridges as designed to prevent their reinforcements from moving north to the Pas de Calais.

Bomber attacks on coastal defence positions were also carefully designed to avoid tipping off the location of the invasion. In this they were successful and while only slight damage was done to the concrete emplacements of the Atlantic Wall, German reports indicate that building materials to extend and complete installations were progressively more difficult to obtain.

A ficticious American Army group, with a busy radio network and General Patton in command, was set up in eastern England. The countryside was dotted with dummy tanks, transports and glider aircraft and preparations for embarking non-existent troops continued through June and July 1944. A landing in the Pas de Calais area fitted into the German General Staff's appreciation that this area offered the Allies the shortest way across the Channel and the best route into Germany; it also flattered Hitler into believing that the Allies considered his 'V' weapons to be so important that they would plan their landings with a view to destroying their launching sites, in the Pas de Calais area, as quickly as possible. So thoroughly convinced was the German High Command that it continued to believe in June and part of July that the Normandy

A Halifax bomber of No. 6 RCAF Group at work over France. CFPU PL 30780

landing was a diversionary attack and it, therefore, refused to weaken the defences in the Pas de Calais area until it was too late to effect the outcome of the battle for Normandy.

The Allied planners were confident that their deception schemes were confusing the enemy. Ultra, the intelligence source based on the decoding of German messages sent by their Enigma machines, kept the Allies informed of broad enemy strategy and provided detailed information on the location of all the main Panzer formations in the west.

The establishment of absolute air and naval superiority in the Channel was a requirement because the size and numbers of the convoys involved in the landing operation would make them very vulnerable targets. The amount of shipping required for the assault and supply was enormous - 4126 landing ships and craft, 864 merchant ships and 736 ancillary ships - a large portion of which sailed virtually simultaneously through well-defined channels which had to be cleared of mines. Any kind of attacker, whether U-boat, surface vessel or aircraft which managed to penetrate the escorts was almost assured of a victim. The extent of the casualties which could be inflicted had been well-illustrated when E-boats had penetrated an escort screen during an American landing exercise in the spring of 1944. They had sunk just two ships but had killed over 700 troops and sailors. At Salerno the intervention of the KG 100 squadron using radio-guided 3000 lb. bombs had seriously damaged four of the Allied warships.

The danger was real and SHAEF demanded and got the largest modern fleet ever assembled, 1213 allied warships including the bombarding squadrons which doubled as escorts, but excluding the distant cover of the Home Fleet which watched for the possible intervention of the larger surface units of the German fleet. The greatest danger remained the German mines, particularly the new pressure mines which were difficult to sweep and for which no proper counter-measures were developed until after a mine had been captured intact on June 9th. Given the size of the target presented, the losses sustained by the huge convoys at the hands of German naval forces were remarkably small.

RCAF photo of damage to a train yard in France. CFPU PL 32257

The Luftwaffe retained, in 1944, a more fearsome reputation than the German navy had ever had. Consequently, control of the airspace over the convoys and the beaches was regarded as essential. For this purpose the Allied Command gathered together an air umbrella of truly gigantic proportions. On D-Day and throughout the 'Neptune' assault phase, SHAEF could employ some 11,590 aircraft (excluding 3,500 gliders) out of the roughly 13,000 operational aircraft stationed in England. An elaborate plan for D-Day was developed which established long-range fighter patrols over areas of France as far east as Calais and as far south as Le Mans - then another continuous screen around the Normandy Peninsula and finally a low and high altitude cover over the beaches and far back to the assembly areas of the convoys off the Isle of Wight; all told 3,700 fighters were committed. There were fighter bombers, rocket-firing Typhoons, twin-engined Mosquitoes and B25's available for close-support, as well as 3,500 heavies of Bomber Command and the 8th US Air Force ready to lay down bomb carpets to overwhelm the defences. The 3rd German Air Force stationed in France had scarcely 200 operational fighters and few bombers; some estimates put the numbers as low as 90 fighters and 70 bombers. In either case, the German Air Force was totally overwhelmed and although it flew a few sorties during the first few days of the invasion, their effect was minimal. In the air, as on the sea, Allied superiority was simply not challengeable.

DIRECTIVE TO SUPREME COMMANDER ALLIED EXPEDITIONARY FORCE

1. You are hereby designated as Supreme Allied Commander of the forces placed under your orders for operations for the liberation of Europe from the Germans. Your title will be Supreme Commander, Allied Expeditionary Force.

2. Task. You will enter the continent of Europe and in conjunction with other United Nations undertake operations aimed at the heart of Germany and the destruction of her armed forces. The date for entering the continent is the month of May, 1944. After adequate channel ports have been secured, exploitation will be directed towards securing an area that will facilitate both ground and air operations against the enemy.

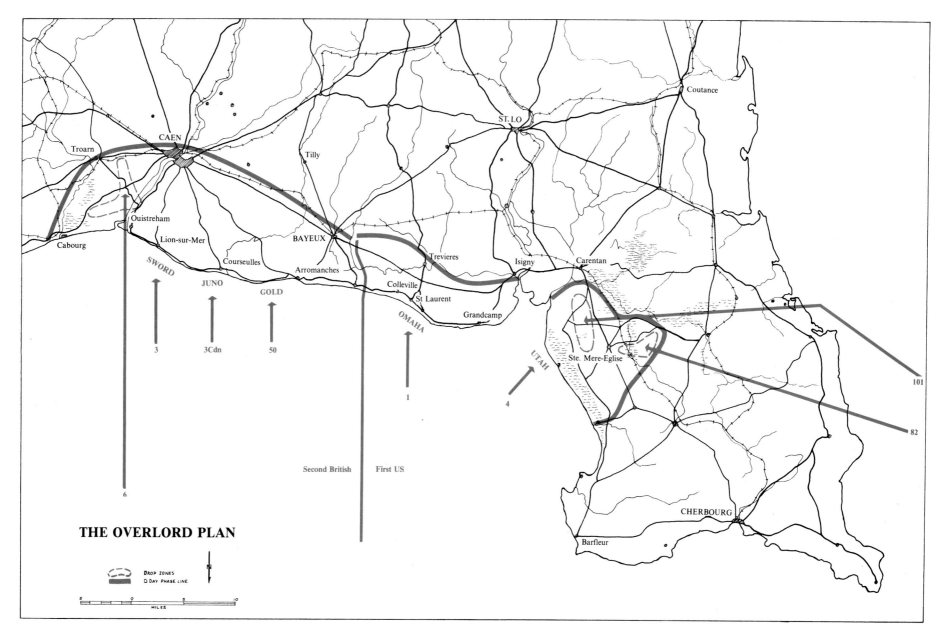

Coutance

ST. LO

CAEN

Troarn

Tilly

Ouistreham

Lion-sur-Mer

BAYEUX

Cabourg

Courseulles

Trevieres

Carentan

SWORD

Arromanches

Isigny

JUNO

GOLD

Colleville

St Laurent

OMAHA

Grandcamp

3

3Cdn

50

UTAH

Ste. Mere-Eglise

101

1

4

82

6

Second British

First US

CHERBOURG

THE OVERLORD PLAN

Barfleur

DROP ZONES

D DAY PHASE LINE

N

5   0   5   10

MILES

The Canadians

Canada's overall contribution to the war effort of the Allied nations was impressive by any standard. By the end of the war more than one million Canadians, including 50,000 women and 41.5 percent of the male population between the ages of 18 and 45, had served in the Armed Forces. Of these, 85 percent were volunteers. The army with more than 700,000 enlistments was by far the largest service, but the Royal Canadian Airforce numbered 222,501 and the Royal Canadian Navy, 99,407.

The Canadians were to play a significant role in Overlord and the campaign in N.W. Europe. No. 6 (RCAF) Bomber Group was first into battle sharing the responsibility for the success of 'Pointblank'. Sixteen RCAF squadrons of the Tactical Air Force were united in No. 83 Group which was to support Second British Army from Normandy to Germany. The Royal Canadian Navy was strongly represented in the 'Neptune' plan. Our destroyers, frigates and corvettes were heavily committed and five RCN landing craft flotillas were training to bring Canadian and British soldiers to the beachhead.

The buildup of the Canadian army overseas was complete by the spring of 1943. The size of the Canadian contingent had led to the establishment of First Canadian Army, composed of two corps containing five divisions, two independent tank brigades and the scores of support units required to make up the largest type of military formation in the Allied armies. First Canadian Army was the creation of General Andrew McNaughton, who was the closest thing to a national hero this country was to have during the war. McNaughton, 'Andy' to the troops, had waged a fierce battle for the autonomy of Canada's army and was firmly opposed to splitting up his forces. When public and political pressure to get the Canadians into action had led the government to ask the British to use a Canadian division in the Mediterranean, McNaughton had agreed on the understanding that it would be returned to him in time for 'Overlord'.

The idea of sending a division to participate in the landings in Sicily made a good deal of sense. Valuable lessons would be learned and the whole army would benefit from the combat experience of the 1st Division. What made no sense at all was the decision to dispatch 5th Armoured Division and the Army's most experienced Corps Headquarters to Italy in the fall of 1943. The British had already begun to transfer divisions from the Mediterranean to Britain for 'Overlord' and the transfer of Canadians in the other direction was both wasteful and profoundly destructive to the morale of the Canadian Army. McNaughton was strongly opposed to the move. Already in conflict with a number of leading British generals he was now completely at odds with the Canadian government. McNaughton was forced to resign and the Canadian Army was forced to remain divided between the two theatres of war.

McNaughton's successor, Lieutenant-General H.D.G. 'Harry' Crerar, possessed none of the charismatic qualities which had made 'Andy' a popular figure. Crerar was intelligent, hard working and well-trained, but he was a shy, private individual and was quite incapable of playing the role of inspirational leader. Guy Granville Simonds, who had led the 1st Division at Sicily and returned to England to assume command of 2nd Canadian Corps, was quite a different type. Simonds was a protégé of Montgomery's, who later described him as 'the best general the Allies produced during the war'. Tall, lean and humourless, Simonds was a forceful and creative soldier with a personality 'as cold as ice'. Everyone respected Simonds but he inspired little affection.

The 3rd Canadian Division had been selected for the Normandy invasion in the summer of 1943. It would form part of Lieutenant General J. T. Crocker's 1st British Corps until the 2nd Canadian Corps was landed in France. The Division was commanded by R.F.L. 'Rod' Keller, an energetic regular army officer who had risen from Major to Major-General since the outbreak of war. At 42, Keller was too young to have seen action in the First World War and he had not taken part in the campaign in Italy. The decision to leave him in command instead of replacing him with a Mediterranean veteran was a tribute to the standard of training and high morale of the entire division.

Division is a military term describing the smallest fighting formation that is tactically and administratively a self-contained unit, capable of independent action. Apart from that concept, anything goes. The 3rd Canadian, like its British counterparts in the assault, was to go ashore in three Brigade Groups composed of three infantry battalions, an armoured regiment, two artillery field regiments, combat engineer companies and a host of specialized units. More than 20,000 men, 200 tanks and hundreds of other vehicles would be under Keller's command.

The three infantry brigade commanders were men in their thirties, RMC graduates but non-permanent militia men before the war. They had gone through the mill of staff college in Britain and their promotions were evidence of their success, but they were as 'green' as their troops. D.G. Cunningham, of the 9th Brigade, had held a staff job in Italy and had survived the landing at Dieppe but as he himself said, 'no one could really call that battle experience'. Brigadier R.A. Wyman who commanded the Division's 2nd Armoured Brigade, had been brought back from Italy where he had led the 1st Armoured Brigade through the Sicily invasion and on into the peninsula.

The core of the 3rd Division, as in all British and Canadian formations, was the battalion. Here was the soldier's home and he seldom gave much thought to his place in higher formations. Each Canadian overseas infantry battalion was in theory simply the active part of a regiment. Canadian regiments were closely modelled on their British counterparts and often shared their names. Even when a purely local title such as the Regina Rifles was chosen, the unit incorporated the traditions of British rifle units and was associated with a sister regiment in Britain. At first recruits were largely drawn from the area where the unit was formed, and friends, brothers and neighbours served together. By the spring of 1944, this regional character was breaking down and it would virtually disappear after a month or two of combat, although the idea of the regiment lived on.

The Lieutenant-Colonel, who commanded the battalion, was in some ways comparable to the captain of a ship of war. He was both a battle

General H.G.D. "Harry" Crerar, G.O.C. 1st Canadian Army.

leader and father figure. The character of the battalion was strongly influenced by his personality. There was no set formula for success. Some battalion commanders were strict disciplinarians, remote from their men but respected for their competence. Others were easy-going, inspirational leaders, who led the troops by personal example and won a loyalty that bonded men into a band of brothers. Most of the Lieutenant-Colonels were men in their early thirties, militia soldiers for whom serious training for war had begun in England. Before the Normandy campaign was over, fourteen battalion commanders would become battle casualties.

Command in the armoured regiments that went ashore with the 3rd Canadian infantry division was more complicated. Second Canadian Armoured Brigade Headquarters provided an administrative core but armoured regiments were assigned to infantry brigades and became closely attached to them. Regiments in turn fought as squadrons attached to infantry battalions. The major or captain who commanded the squadron, controlled five troops of three or four tanks and worked more closely with his infantry battalion than his regimental commander. Despite this, armoured regiments were fiercely united, confident of their superiority and special skills, convinced that no foot soldier could really understand the proper role of the tank.

Except for the Royal Canadian Artillery, the other supporting arms and services were attached to infantry units or part of divisional troops. The 'gunners' even when detached as a 'battery' to work with a battalion, remained gunners; masters of the complex mysteries of the 'shoot' - the scientists of the battlefield.

During the first months of 1944, the Canadians, like the other assault units, found themselves caught up in a training programme which became more and more detailed. The plans for 'Overlord' filled volumes of paper, all stamped 'Bigot', the special, super top-secret code for the invasion. Apart from the exercises, it was a staff officer's war. No detail was too small. Decisions were made about how much rum, (whiskey for officers and NCO's), should be carried and where. The battle gear of the individual soldier was weighed, assessed, reduced, weighed again. Gas

Winston Churchill is invited to lunch. PA 129046/Public Archives Canada.

respirators were discarded by some brigades, carried by others. Would one or two 24-hour ration packs be necessary? Eye shields for troops who had to ride on tanks, were issued. Other equipment identified in that marvelously precise military terminology as 'Knives fighting', 'Paint Phospherence Luminous', 'Tape Tracing' and 'Jerkins assault' was indented for.

Experiments on waterproofing vehicles produced good results but 246 man hours per vehicle were needed to accomplish it and practice in de-waterproofing was required. Folding bicycles were a much-debated item and it was decided that the soldiers of the reserve brigades would carry them. (Most soldiers carried the bikes as far as the beach before dumping them.) The planners planned and the soldiers rehearsed.

How they did rehearse! Squadrons of the First Hussars and Fort Garry Horse went off to school to learn to navigate their DD tanks. The Divisional staff officers were in London for a month mastering the plan. On April 12th, Exercise 'Trousers' took the division through the first stage of the landing. Then, in early May, 'Force J' and the 3rd Canadian Division assaulted the long-suffering coastline of the south of England in Exercise Fabius III which closely simulated the plan for the first two days of the campaign. As the troops headed for the sealed embarkation area to receive their final briefings, there was a collective sigh of relief that at least the rehearsals were over.

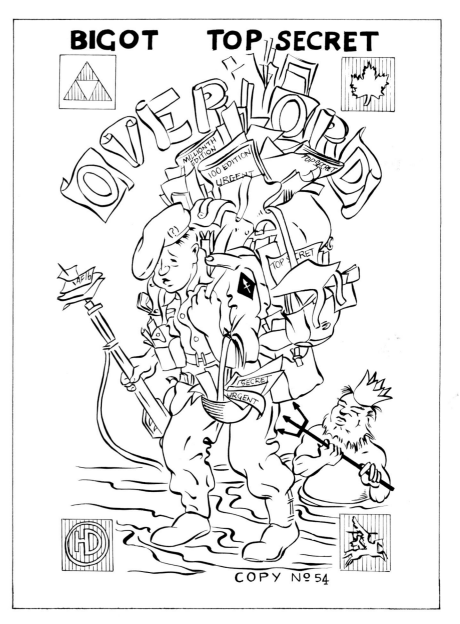

An anonymous staff officer's view of Overlord preparations. The four shoulder patches of 1st British Corps are illustrated with a maple leaf superimposed on the grey rectangle of 3rd Canadian Division.

The senior officers of 3rd Canadian Division Photographed in France, June 25, 1944. Front Row (2nd from left to right) Brig. R.A. Wyman, Brig. H.W. Foster, General Keller, General Crocker, Brig. P.A.S. Todd, Brig. K.G. Blackader, Brig. D.G. Cunningham.
PA 129038/Public Archives Canada

General Bernard Montgomery addressing Canadian troops March 1, 1944. Montgomery spent much of his time in the pre-invasion months visiting every formation which was to take part in Overlord.
PA 129049/Public Archives Canada.

Operation Neptune

The assault on the Atlantic Wall promised to be a fearsome enterprise. It had all the characteristics of an attack on a fortified position that had caused such terrible casualties in the First World War. The Germans had had two years to build a modern fortification system. A series of reinforced concrete gun-emplacements, supported by well-protected infantry strong-points overlooked the beaches which were strewn with ingenious obstacles and minefields. The Allied convoys would either have to unload their cargoes within range of the coastal batteries or so far out to sea that it would take the smaller landing craft several hours to reach the beaches. To enable the landing craft to avoid the worst obstacles, the landing had to take place before high tide, making it necessary for the soldiers to cross several hundred yards of open, mined beaches swept by the fire of automatic weapons. There was no way back if the Atlantic Wall could not be breached. It would be virtually impossible to lift the troops off the beaches and re-embark them in the ships. Certainly the casualties would be astronomical and the heavy equipment would have to be abandoned. Whatever the success of the preliminary weakening of the defences had been, whatever the brilliance of the plans for a break out from the beachhead might be, the critical moment was still the breaching of the shore-line defences and the establishment of a viable foothold on the mainland.

The preliminary steps - the deception plan, the disruption of the transportation system and the build-up of Allied naval and air supremacy had been completed by the end of May 1944. There remained the question of the softening up of the defences immediately before and during the actual assault.

For this purpose, the Allied Command believed that it would be necessary first to land air-borne divisions on both flanks of the invasion front in order to confuse the enemy and to prevent him from reinforcing his coastal defences immediately. Secondly, the strong points would have to be smothered with an air and naval bombardment of momentous proportions. Finally, the infantry would have to be supported with a sufficient number of armoured vehicles to protect them during the crossing of the beaches and to provide them with immediately available fire power to overcome the local resistance nests.

The use of air-borne divisions had caused considerable debate. Large air-borne operations had not had unqualified success during the war and even the successful ones, such as the German conquest of Crete, had incurred unacceptably high casualties. It seemed dangerous to rely too heavily on the success of such a hazardous enterprise. Some thought it would be wiser to use these highly trained divisions to exploit success rather than to avoid disaster. Nevertheless, 'Neptune' called for the use of three air-borne divisions, the US 82nd and 101st to be dropped on the right flank, immediately ahead of 'Utah' beach in order to control the roads to the beaches and to facilitate the link-up of the troops between the two US assault beaches. The 6th British Air-borne Division would be dropped on the left flank in order to control the bridges across the Orne River, to destroy the Merville Battery just across the river from 'Sword' beach and generally to prevent the Germans from moving troops against the flank of the British beaches.

SHAEF had to devise an intricate timetable for the bombardment planned for the night of June 5th-6th. The transport aircraft of the air-borne divisions had to avoid the flight path of the heavy bombers and the final light bomber sweep had to be timed so as to avoid confusing the naval artillery. There had to be sufficient flexibility to enable guns and air-support to be quickly brought to bear on unexpected or especially tough German strong points. Thousands of small calibre rockets fired from especially adapted landing-craft had to hit the beaches simultaneously in order to explode a large number of mines, that were part of the defence perimeter.

The naval artillery was to be directed by a spotter aircraft one for each of the larger warships, each with its own protective fighter plane. Naval liaison officers were attached to ground units so that they could call for naval fire on particular targets ahead of the advancing infantry. Airforce liaison officers were attached to call for the support of the tactical

Air Marshall Coningham visits his Canadian squadrons. CFPU PL 30185

airforce. The communications systems, centered on the HQ ships lying off-shore had to be enormously sophisticated and efficient to avoid confusion and disasterous accidents.

The provision of armoured vehicles presented a serious problem. It was impossible to imagine that the infantry could cross the beaches and breach the Atlantic Wall successfully without their presence. The difficulty, of course, was getting them onto the beaches and unloading them so quickly that they would not become easy targets for the shore guns. For this purpose a great variety of specialized ships had to be built, large ocean going vessels which could quickly transfer troops and tanks into smaller landing craft which were also part of their cargo. The landing ships, moreover, had to have shallow droughts so as to be able to approach the beaches and unload directly when the situation warranted.

The smaller craft were flat-bottomed, could carry between four and eight medium tanks which could be discharged from them by means of a ramp. The invasion fleet contained a huge variety of such craft and ships of which nearly 47,000 were built during the war. Still they were mostly slow, vulnerable and very hard to manoeuvre and the most desirable solution was still an amphibious tank which could be launched from an LST (Landing Ship, Tank) which was anchored fairly far out to sea.

The DD tank was a partial solution. It was a Sherman tank, waterproofed with a collapsible canvas screen around the hull, which was strengthened by easily installable struts. Two propellers, which moved the vehicle through water, could be attached to the engine of the tank. The tank hung suspended underneath a kind of square canvas boat. When the tracks grounded on the beach the crew, usually sitting on the tank rather than it it, easily dismantled the canvas screen, and were ready to fight. While in the water these machines were awkward and easily swamped if the sea was rough. Nevertheless, the DD tanks made up the front line as the assault forces moved towards the beaches.

There was need for other armoured vehicles. A whole British armoured division, the 79th and the Royal Engineers had been given the task of devising a variety of specialised vehicles which could clear minefields, drop fascines into anti-tank ditches, lay bridges, generally, in fact, perform the myriad engineering and sapper tasks of the battlefield from the inside of an armoured vehicle. They would arrive on the beaches in LCT's (Landing Craft, Tank) immediately behind the DD tanks and they would clear the mines and open the way for the other tanks by laying paths across ditches and streams. Many of them were also able to offer fire support to the infantry; in fact throughout the campaign that followed, specialized tanks would be used over and over again whenever a major fortification had to be taken or a river crossed. The tank had become an indispensible part of the battlefield and it had to be present from the very first moment of the landings in sufficient numbers to support the infantry in breaking through the shore defences.

The actual date of the invasion was determined by the correct combination of moon and tide. Only a few days in each month were suitable and the weather also had to be reasonably good. The unexpectedly bad weather on June 4th-5th brought a postponement of one day, although even then the seas were expected to be running so high that the smaller boats would have a difficult passage. It was a remarkable tribute to the naval organization that despite the weather, it was possible to recall the many convoys already at sea and re-assemble them so they could be sailed again in the right order, within a few hours. The midget submarines, X 20 and X 23, whose duty it was to guide the forces on 'Juno' and 'Sword' beaches by flashing a green light from close inshore, could not be recalled and had to lie just off the Normandy coast for the whole of Monday, June 5th.

During the night of June 5th-6th the enormous weight of Allied sea and airpower was brought to bear on the roughly fifty-five miles of coastline which made up the invasion front. Air activity increased all along that front before midnight and then a few minutes past midnight, the air-borne troops began their descent on Normandy. Both British and US air-landings ran into the usual problems of planes loosing their way and men and equipment becoming separated. In the dark, company and battalion commanders found it difficult to gather their men together and to locate their objectives. Despite this confusion and considerable loss of strength, the main tasks allotted to these divisions were fulfilled. The US divisions established themselves in the area in front of 'Utah' beach, while the British staked out a claim on the eastern side of the Orne river which would not have to be given up again. Some of the further objectives were not held but considerable damage was done. The Canadian 1st Parachute Battalion was part of the British 6th Air Borne Division's 3rd Brigade and its 'C' company landed in the most easterly drop-zone near Varville. There it had the task of blowing up a bridge across the Divetter River, destroying a German strong-point and then moving back about four miles to le Mesnil, a village at an important junction of the east-west, north-south highways. 'B' company had the task of blowing up the bridge at Robehomme and then concentrating in the le Mesnil area.

All these major tasks were fulfilled; in fact three other bridges were destroyed and the concentration with the other sections of the 3rd Brigade effected. The troops landing on 'Sword' beach linked up with the air-borne units in the area of the Benouville-Ranville bridges in the first hours after the landing. The possession of these bridges and the le Mesnil road junction would force German reinforcements from the east to use the road through Troarn and Caen which meant considerable delay in reaching the front north of Caen. Despite high casualties, the air-borne divisions brought confusion to the German defences and thereby facilitated the landings.

To further confuse the enemy, dummy air-landings were made in a variety of areas, all of which had to be investigated by the German ground forces before they could be sure that they were indeed fakes. 'Windows' were dropped to confuse the German radar and small boats towing large balloons which looked like incoming ships on the radar screens made runs towards the Pas de Calais and the lower Seine coastline.

Her Majesty Queen Elizabeth and Princess Elizabeth inspect a member of 1st Canadian Parachute Battalion, 6th Airborne Division in full combat-camouflage gear.
PA 129047/Public Archives Canada.

The heavy bombers had already bombed the batteries and the strong-points which were among the objectives of the air-borne troops and then between 0315 hours when the first wave of air-drops had been completed, and 0500 hours, the seven most important enemy batteries came under attack. More than a thousand bombers dropped five thousand tons of bombs on these targets. When the last bombers left it was beginning to get light and at 0530 hours the fleet, having taken up its bombarding position, opened fire on the twenty-six German gun-emplacements which stretched from Villerville to Barfleur. Each ship had its own particular target and the enormous weight of shell-fire disrupted, even if it did not always destroy, the German gun positions.

For the Canadian and the British troops this was one of the most dangerous moments because the big transports had anchored to lower the assault craft. The transports were stopped only seven miles from the coast, well within range of the German batteries. The US assault forces had elected to unload eleven miles out to sea, out of range of the guns but this decision increased the time required to reach the shore by almost an hour. It turned out to be a mistake, for the enemy guns were largely suppressed by the naval gun-fire and the rough sea caused greater damage amongst the boats and the DD tanks than did the German batteries.

Another wave of aircraft swept in to add a final bombing of the shore defences. Low cloud, however, forced the aircraft to drop their bombs further inland to avoid the possibility of hitting the landing craft and consequently this last attack appears to have been largely ineffective.

Finally, as the landing craft moved in lines towards the beaches, some fifty-six destroyers took up position on their flanks and began firing towards the shore. Landing craft with self-propelled artillery added high-trajectory fire to the high-velocity, flat-trajectory fire from the naval guns. Five minutes before H-hour, the moment of touch-down of the assault craft, thousands of rockets deluged the beaches and exploded a large number of mines laid on the beaches. As the fearsome noise died away, the DD tanks and the small landing craft grounded along the shores of Normandy.

Four years previously, almost to the day, the small ships of the British fleet had disappeared westwards across the Channel carrying the last soldiers without their equipment from the smoke-choked beaches of Dunkirk; now they loomed out of the morning mists, bringing back to France the most modern mechanized armies which the arsenals of democracy could provide.

Canadian Tribal Destroyers Leaving on Patrol, Plymouth by Tony Law (10249). There were four "Tribals" HMCS Athabaskan, Haida, Huron and Iroquois. Athabaskan was sunk in action against German forces during April. Haida and Huron were involved in the major naval battle of Operation Neptune, June 9th, which resulted in the destruction of two German destroyers and damage to two others.

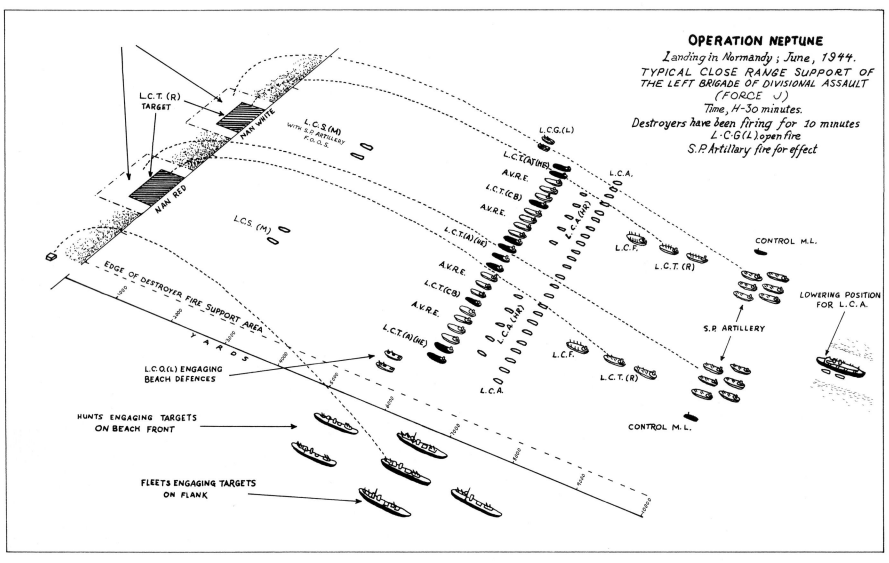

OPERATION NEPTUNE

Landing in Normandy ; June, 1944.

TYPICAL CLOSE RANGE SUPPORT OF
THE LEFT BRIGADE OF DIVISIONAL ASSAULT
(FORCE J)

Time, H-30 minutes.

Destroyers have been firing for 10 minutes
L.C.G.(L). open fire

S.P. Artillery fire for effect

L.C.T. (R)
TARGET

NAN WHITE

L.C.S. (M)
WITH S.P. ARTILLERY
F.O.O.S.

NAN RED

L.C.S. (M)

L.C.G.(L)

L.C.T.(A)(HE)

A.V.R.E.

L.C.T.(CB)

A.V.R.E.

L.C.A.

L.C.A.(HR)

CONTROL M.L.

L.C.F.

L.C.T. (R)

L.C.T.(A)(HE)

L.C.A.(HR)

LOWERING POSITION
FOR L.C.A.

EDGE OF DESTROYER FIRE SUPPORT AREA

A.V.R.E.

L.C.T.(CB)

A.V.R.E.

L.C.T.(A)(HE)

Y A R D S

1000
2000
3000
4000
5000
6000
7000
8000
9000
10000

S.P. ARTILLERY

L.C.F.

L.C.T. (R)

L.C.Q.(L) ENGAGING
BEACH DEFENCES

L.C.A.

CONTROL M.L.

HUNTS ENGAGING TARGETS
ON BEACH FRONT

FLEETS ENGAGING TARGETS
ON FLANK

32

HMCS Sioux one of the Canadian Destroyers which provided close support on D-Day.
PA 115559/Public Archives Canada.

A Canadian Army Chaplain Captain Seaburn, offers prayers with Engineer troops before embarking. PA 129054/Public Archives Canada

Landing Craft Assault carrying 8th Brigade to the beaches of Bernieres.
PA 129058/Public Archives Canada

Invasion Pattern, Normandy
by Eric Aldwinckle. (10679)

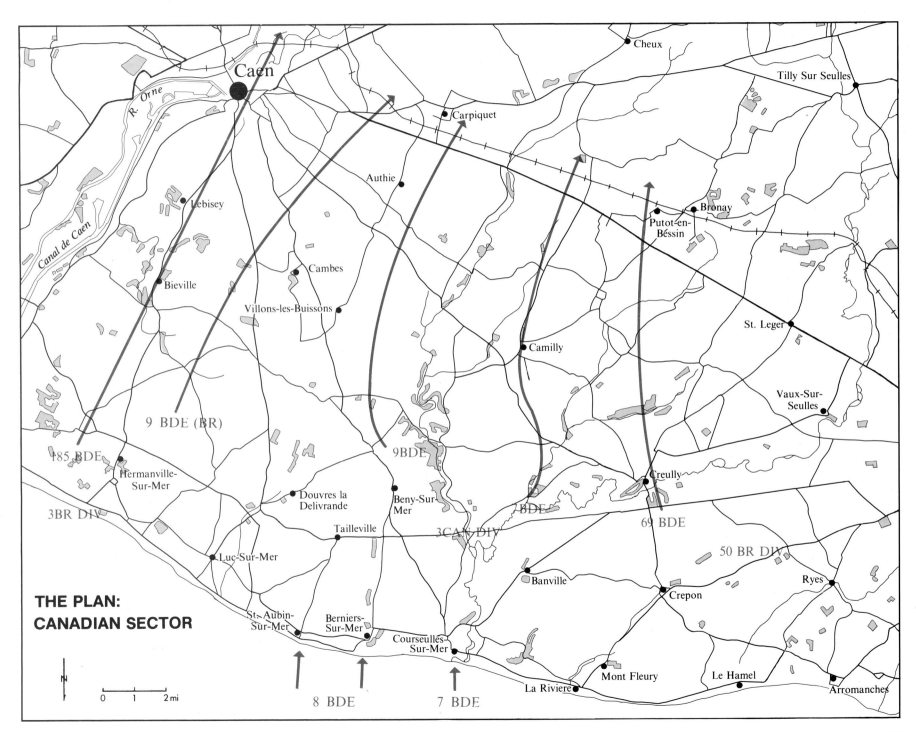

Cheux

Tilly Sur Seulles

Caen

R. Orne

Carpiquet

Bronay

Lebisey

Authie

Putot-en-Béssin

Canal de Caen

Cambes

Bieville

Villons-les-Buissons

St. Leger

9 BDE (BR)

Camilly

Vaux-Sur-Seulles

185 BDE

9BDE

Hermanville-Sur-Mer

Creully

3BR DIV

Douvres la Delivrande

Beny-Sur-Mer

7 BDE

69 BDE

Tailleville

3CAN DIV

50 BR DIV

Luc-Sur-Mer

Banville

Ryes

Crepon

**THE PLAN:
CANADIAN SECTOR**

St. Aubin-Sur-Mer

Berniers-Sur-Mer

Courseulles-Sur-Mer

La Riviere

Mont Fleury

Le Hamel

Arromanches

N

0   1   2 mi

8 BDE

7 BDE

The 8th Brigade Landings

The North Shore (New Brunswick) Regiment's orders were to: 'capture beach position, mop up St. Aubin, form the left flank of the Brigade position and a firm base for the 48 Royal Marine Commando to capture Langrune. When 48 Royal Marine Commando has passed through. NSR will capture Tailleville'. Later in the day, assuming success, the New Brunswickers were to move on to take the radar station at Douvres.

The run-in went smoothly with the 105 mm guns of the 14th and 19th Field Regiments firing a steady barrage for the crucial thirty minutes before the touchdown. The Fort Garry's amphibious tanks were not launched at the 7000 yard point because of sea conditions. Instead the LCT's came within 2000 yards of the shore. 'The Launch' the unit's War Diary records, 'was really a wet wade', though the screens had to be inflated and propellers engaged. Both infantry and armour landed within minutes of each other and found the beach 'fairly quiet except for sniping'. The first wave of infantry raced across the beach with 'only a few casualties'. 'A' Company broke through on the western edge of the village, clearing houses with caution once the first booby-trap was encountered. It was able to report 'Yew' the initial objective along the coast road at 0948 hours. Getting there had cost 'A' Company 24 casualties.

'B' Company drew St. Aubin proper and the encased strong point in the village. After the first breathless rush across the sand, 'B' Company was faced with an appalling situation. Neither the air nor the naval bombardment appeared to have hit St. Aubin and 'certainly did not touch the assigned target, a special strong point'. The artillery had performed its primary task of keeping the enemy's heads down during the actual landing, but had done little actual damage to the defenders. The Fort Garry tanks fired steadily from their beach positions waiting for the specialized armour to clear an exit through a minefield. The infantry pushed into the village and tried to overcome the strong point while sniper fire harrassed the scattered sections.

The reserve companies began landing at 0945 to find much heavier fire

directed at the narrowing beach strip. There was now a good deal of confusion and still no exit for the tanks. Major Bray, in command of 'C' Squadron, gave up waiting for the engineers and forced his way through the minefield losing three tanks in the attempt. The 13 tanks still available worked closely with the infantry and St. Aubin was soon under control except for the strong point. Tanks, infantry and engineers with Petard tanks struggled to subdue the position most of the morning. The defenders not only held up the North Shores but helped to close Nan Red beach to further landing craft. The 50 mm gun was finally dealt with four hours after landing and 48 prisoners were taken. Even then a handful of diehards fought on until late in the evening.

The Queen's Own Rifles landing at Nan White beach had the roughest experience of all the Canadian battalions. The DD tanks were so late that they played no role in overcoming the first line of resistance. The AVRE's were also well behind the infantry and Team 2 which was to help overcome the Bernieres 'Resistance Nest' landed some 300 yards east of its objective. If this was not bad enough 'B' Company of the QOR's was put ashore directly in front of the 'Resistance Nest' instead of 200 yards to the west of the main defensive position. The men of 'B' Company had to draw on unknown reserves of courage and endurance to save the situation. Three men, Lieutenant Herbert, Lance-Corporal Tessier and Rifleman Chicosk, were awarded medals for their attack on the main pillbox. Their mad dash across the sand was a superhuman achievement on a morning when extraordinary bravery was commonplace.

'A' Company came in well to the west of the strongpoint and got off the beach quickly but was held up at the railway line by heavy, accurate mortar fire. With the capture of the 'Resistance Nest' by 'B' Company and renewal of the advance by 'A', Bernieres was largely secure before 9:00 a.m. Just about everything that could go wrong had gone wrong on Nan White beach but the infantry had come through.

The QOR's reserve companies and the reserve battalion, the Régiment de la Chaudière, suffered heavily for the delays which the weather had imposed on the timing of the assault. By 0845 when the second wave of

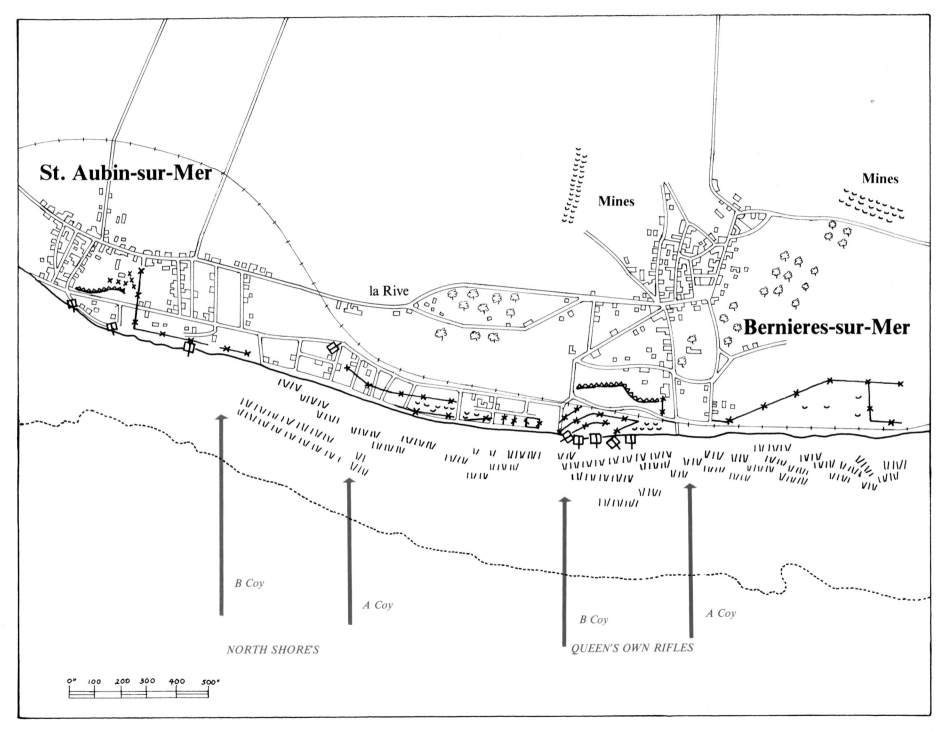

St. Aubin-sur-Mer

la Rive

Mines

Mines

Bernieres-sur-Mer

B Coy

A Coy

B Coy

A Coy

NORTH SHORE'S

QUEEN'S OWN RIFLES

0ʸ 100 200 300 400 500ʸ

the QOR's arrived, the tide had covered many of the mined obstacles and a number of landing craft were hit. At 0930 when the 'Chauds' were landing, the beach had narrowed to a small strip and one RCN flotilla, carrying 'A' Company of the Chaudieres, suffered damage to four of its five LCA's. Most of the troops swam to shore losing much of their equipment.

The Chaudieres waited behind the beach wall trying to re-organize while the QOR's dealt with the last diehards in Bernieres. The 'Chauds' then moved through the town to their assembly area greeted everywhere by locals amazed to hear them speak French. By 10:30 a.m. the tanks and 'Priests' (self-propelled artillery) were ashore linking up with the Chaudieres for the advance inland. The 8th Brigade had broken through the Atlantic Wall!

"Nan Red" Beach at St.
Aubin-la Rive, late morning
June 6th, 1944.
CFPU PL 14480/81

The North Shores.....

Lt. 'Bones' McCann commanded No. 6 platoon. 'Our run-in was not bad,' he said, 'except for a few of the lads suffering from mal-de-mer. Jerry, apparently aiming for bigger targets and apart from small arms fire, and shelling, we landed as per schedule and intact. Some of my fellow officers were not so fortunate and because of this things really began to happen. Unknown to me, Lt. Gerry Moran had been seriously wounded on the beach and shortly I was in charge of two platoons instead of one, and could have used six for after cutting our way with bangalore torpedoes and wire cutters into the village our communications broke down, and it was during this period that we found that the guns and emplacement that were to have been put out of business by the air force were intact and very much in use. Also that Jerry had a beautiful underground system of communicating with his pillboxes. Perhaps it was well we didn't know everything for, working on the assumption that we had a pushover, we went into the village in nothing flat. Now came the test. Things weren't going as planned and unless we captured those heavy guns Jerry was potting landing craft with, things were going to get worse. And worse they got, for there we were with nothing heavier than Brens with which to attack heavily-fortified enemy posts.

Lt. G. V. Moran had No. 5 platoon and said that as they approached the beach they came under small-arms fire depressed to ground level. 'Frank Ryan was the first man ashore from our craft followed by his section of six men, then myself with platoon headquarters and the other two sections. We were not too interested in looking around to see whether anyone else had landed or not but reached the doubtful shelter of the sea wall. It would be hard to estimate the width of the beach, but since the tide was well out I would hazard a guess of 300 feet at the time of our landing, and every square inch buzzed with small-arms fire. The sea wall offered some protection from straight ahead but not from enfilade fire from the houses up and down the beach, and since there were no troops landing on our immediate left to keep the enemy occupied, they threw everything at us. All officers with the assault carried rifles and wore the same gear as the troops so as not to be conspicious to snipers.

'Too many of us had bunched behind the sea wall and the second wave was coming ashore. In order to get the men moving to their objective, I stood in the open and shouted at the top of my voice and, making vigorous motions with my arms, urged the sections around the wall and forward, standing with my back toward the upper beach and 'A' Company's position. Apparently a sniper in the upper part of a house in 'A' Company's area was watching for just such an indication of authority and laid a sight on the middle of my back. At the instant he squeezed the trigger fate invited me to turn, facing the water, so that I met the bullet with my left arm instead of my back. The slug passed through my arm, entered my chest under my armpit and plowed on, coming out through the middle of my back. I didn't know this at the time because a mortar shell landed by at the same instant and I spun around and fell flat on my face. Rising again, I discovered my left arm useless. Someone pulled me down and I didn't stand again for a month. By this time things had gone hazy and that amazing team of Doc Patterson and Father Hickey were soon at hand.'

The beach at St. Aubin-sur-Mer photographed in 1946. The 50 mm gun position in the foreground was part of the strong point attacked by the North Shore Regiment D-Day. DND PMR 82-083.

Looking out from a German gun position at Bernieres. PA 128792/Public Archives Canada.

Instructions regarding
preparation of War
Diaries; are contained in
F.S. Regs. Vol. 1.

WAR DIARY

Original, duplicate and
triplicate to be forward-
ed to O. i/c 2nd
Echelon for disposal.

Queen's Own Rifles

0315 hrs.	*Breakfast served all who wish it given good shot of navy rum.*
0600 hrs.	*Men file silently to respective boats, before long quite a few are sick due to water's roughness, needless to say the M.O. Capt. Kirsch is right up at the head of the list 7 miles off coast intermittent gun fire but nothing tremendous has developed yet.*
0715 hrs.	*All hell breaks loose as arty and various support weapons cut loose. Shore can now be seen but it is fast becoming obscured.*
0720 hrs.	*H. Hour postponed 30 minutes. DD tanks and AVRE's behind schedule. Up to 0745 no sign of action on beach but now anti-tank shells begin to drop around L.C.A's which makes heads go down in fast order. Unfortunately postponement has definitely messed up support fire and all that is firing now is an LSF which cruised right in close to shore and let loose with a lot of tracers.*
0805 hrs.	*Assault companies go in. As yet no DD's or AVRE's can be seen which looks ominous.*
0815 hrs.	*A & B coys touchdown. B immediately catches a packet of trouble as they are landed in front of a heavily defended position. Several of the LCA's of both companies are blown up by mines but only the front two or three men are injured. A Company are a little better off than B, able to get off the beach. As soon as they hit the railway they come under heavy mortar fire and are pinned down. Casualties mount Lt. Rea wounded. Sgt. Charles Smith extradites platoon. Balance of A Company get through. B Company finally outflanks position.*
0830 hrs.	*C and D coys and alternate B HQ touch down. Casualties among LCA's heavy. Almost one-half blown up by underwater mines. Personnel get ashore and pass through assault companies.*
0900 hrs.	*The support all around has been very disappointing - none of the beach defenses have been touched and this caused very high casualties among the assault companies.*
0940 hrs.	*B HQ arrives. At this time it is noted that a cafe just 100 yards off the beach is opened up and selling wine to all and sundry.*
	Considerable delay as companies assemble. B coy. casualties so heavy they gather first off the beach and try to sort themselves out. A Coy moves to the Forming Up Place. Regiment de Chaudiere has now landed but are prevented from passing through us by the very accurate fire of a battery of 88 guns located just south of Bernieres.

Le Régiment de la Chaud-
ière wait behind the seawall
at Bernieres.
PA 116352/Public Archives
Canada.

*German prisoners at the Bernieres Railway Station.
PA 128790/Public Archives Canada*

The 7th Brigade Landings

On both Allied and German war maps the port of Courseulles-sur-Mer was classified as a 'strong point' containing one 75 mm gun, one 88 mm, and three 50 mm anti-tank guns. Two additional 75 mm guns posted on the flanks covered the approaches on both sides of the town. Most of these positions were protected by concrete. Twelve machine gun pillboxes and two 50 mm mortar emplacements thickened the defences. Courseulles was the most heavily fortified position attacked by the Anglo-Canadian forces on D-Day.

The planners had decided that this formidable position would have to be attacked frontally, presumably because any delay in capturing the main guns would jeopardize the follow-up landings. The Regina Rifle Regiment was assigned the area east of the river, Nan Green beach. The Reginas with 'B' Squadron of the First Hussars came ashore shortly after 8:00 o'clock. The DD tanks launched at 4000 yards in a very rough sea. Major J. S. Duncan who had to make the decision reported that he 'was convinced our chances were good and that failure on our part to launch might seriously affect the operation'. Duncan's own tank was sunk when its flotation gear collapsed but '14 tanks touched down on the proper beach..... well in advance of either AVRE's or infantry..... They immediately went into action against the beach defences'.

'A' Company had to assault the main defences of Courseulles which had been hit by the bombardment but not seriously damaged. Neither Centaurs nor AVRE Petards had arrived and the operational DD tanks were off to the left. 'A' Company suffered heavily in their attack but they were finally able to get tank support and subdue the position by a flanking movement. Unfortunately some of the defenders had gone to ground and when 'A' Company moved on they came under renewed fire and had to turn back to clear the position once again.

'B' Company had a far easier task. Their assault was directed against the pillboxes which were strung-out along the Promenade to the east of Courseulles. With good support from the DD tanks they got off the beach quickly and were able to clear three blocks of Courseulles while 'A' Company was working on the strong point. AVRE's had opened beach exits and the Hussars were able to get their tanks into Courseulles to help the infantry.

The incoming tide was covering many of the mined beach obstacles when the Regina's reserve units landed. 'C' Company got ashore without mishap and moved quickly into the town, but 'D' Company ran into mines which shattered the landing craft. Only 49 survivors made it to shore but somehow they gathered themselves together and set off inland with a squadron of tanks for Reviers, their first objective.

West of the River Seulles 'B' Company of the Royal Winnipeg Rifles came under heavy fire well before their landing craft beached directly in front of the strong point. There was no sign of the DD tanks or AVRE's and one can only marvel at the courage displayed by the troops who waded into shore, rushed across the sand and began the attack on the machine gun and mortar positions. When the DD tanks arrived, the main gun emplacements were taken 'by close range tank fire'. The Winnipegs then pressed on across a bridge into the 'island' formed by the bend in the River Seulles and cleared it of the enemy. 'B' Company and the assault team of 6th Field Company, Royal Canadian Engineers, which had worked with them, had one of the highest casualty rates of D-Day. Captain Gower, the company commander, was left with just 26 men at the end of the day.

Once again the contrast between the experiences of companies in the same regiment was illustrated by good fortune which attended 'D' Company's landing. Coming in to the west of the strongpoint these troops moved off the beach quickly and were able to clear a path through the La Valette minefield. They were equally successful at clearing Graye-sur-Mer allowing the two reserve companies to move through their positions. 'C' Company soon captured Banville but 'A' Company found that Ste. Croix-sur-Mer was strongly defended by a company of the 716th Division which was well dug in.

'C' Company of the Canadian Scottish had been attached to the Winnipegs to extend their flank and to assault a 75 mm gun position

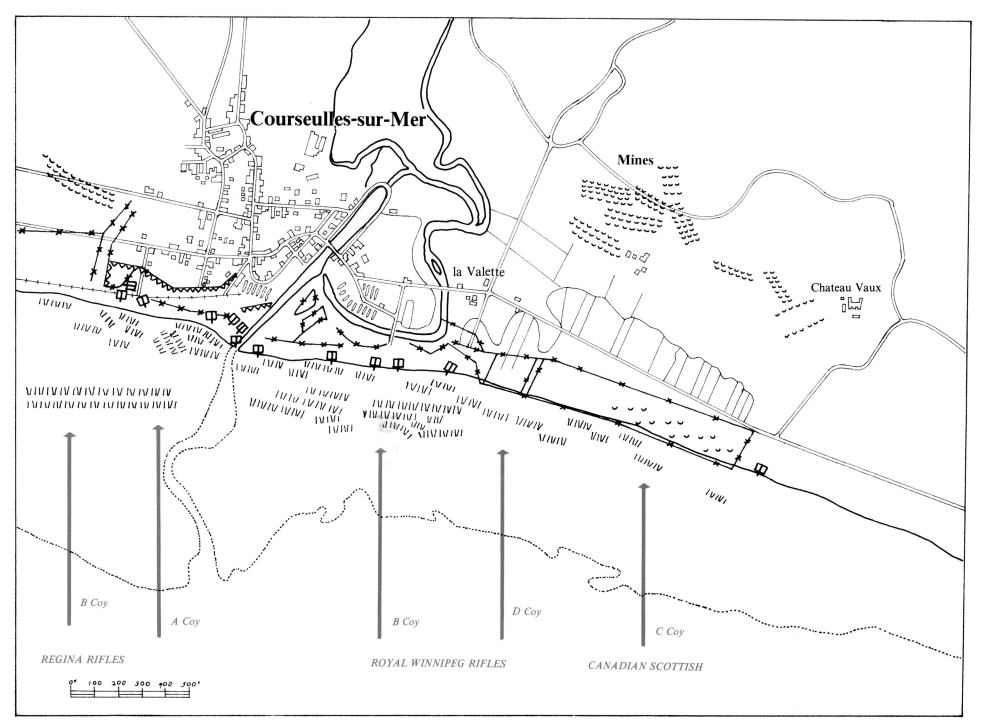

Courseulles-sur-Mer

Mines

la Valette

Chateau Vaux

B Coy

A Coy

B Coy

D Coy

C Coy

REGINA RIFLES

ROYAL WINNIPEG RIFLES

CANADIAN SCOTTISH

0ʸ 100 200 300 400 500ʸ

COURSEULLE - SUR - MER

MAP SHEET:- GSGS. 4250 7E/5 1/50,000

MAP REF:- T.9685

SORTIE:- 400/187   30 MAR. 44.

Air photo of Courseulles with the defences marked in. CFU PL 144857.

which was three quarters of a mile west of the Courseulles strong point. This objective had been put out of action by naval gunfire and the Scottish were able to move on to their second target, the Chateau Vaux, where a dispirited group of Germans surrendered after several grenades were tossed inside.

The three remaining companies of the CSR reached the beach an hour later. It was still under mortar fire and the exits were far from complete. Captain Ramsay of 'B' Company did not wait; he scrambled across an AVRE which had sunk in the flooded area beyond the sand dunes and jumped into knee deep water covering a submerged road. The rest of the Company soon followed and gradually the reserve battalion organized itself to spearhead the advance inland. There was still scattered resistance in the area behind the beaches and problems in Ste. Croix, but at 1200 hours Brigadier Harry Foster could confidently report that the beach was secure.

The beach attacked by 'C' Company the Canadian Scottish. CFPU PL 144864

Instructions regarding
preparation of War
Diaries; are contained in
F.S. Regs. Vol. 1.

WAR DIARY

Original, duplicate and
triplicate to be forward-
ed to O. i/c 2nd
Echelon for disposal.

Royal Winnipeg Rifles

June 6, 0400 hrs.	*Tea and cold snack served.*
0515 hrs.	*LCA's manned and lowered 10 miles off coast.*
0655 hrs.	*Not a shot from shore; Royal Navy and arty bombardment opens up with the SP guns firing short as usual.*
0749 hrs.	*In spite of air bombardment failing to materialize, RN bombardment spotty, the rockets falling short and the AVRE's and D.D.'s being late. 'C' Company C.S.R. ... R.W.R. companies landed all within seven minutes.*
0900 hrs.	*The bombardment having failed to kill a single German or silence one weapon these companies had to storm their positions 'cold' and did so without hesitation.*
1800 hrs.	*'D' Company had by this time gapped a minefield at La Valette and cleared Graye Sur Mer. 'B' Company crossed Seulles, cleared out 4 positions on the island ... 'A' coy started inland 0805 towards St. Croix pinned by 6 to 8 mgs. 'C' coy approached Banville pinned down by 3 mgs. on commanding ground.*

It is desired to make a special note of the services rendered to the Bn during the first day of ops by our MO (Capt Robert M. Caldwell) and the Bn RAP Staff - and the assault sec of 14 Cdn Fd Amb u/c Capt Harry Dixon. Not only were the wounded cared for with skill and despatch but confidence was developed and morale increased accordingly. A very special note, too, should be made about the general tone of the Bn during this day called D - 6 Jun 44. Not one man flinched from his task, no matter how tough it was - not one officer failed to display courage and energy and a degree of gallantry. It is thought that the Little Black Devils, by this days success, has managed to maintain the tradition set by former members. Casualties for the day exceeded 130.

THE ROYAL WINNIPEG RIFLES A.F.
(LITTLE BLACK DEVILS)
IN THE FIELD

R W R 5-0
25 Jun 44

HQ 7 Cdn Inf Bde,
Cdn Army Overseas

6 Cdn Armd Regt

It is desired to bring to attention the outstanding services rendered to this Bn by 6 Cdn Armd Regt during the assault and advance inland on D Day.

In the assault on the beach defences of MIKE Sector A Sqn commanded by Maj Dudley Brooks, literally made possible the overwhelming of the defences. It will be recalled that the pre-assault bombardment had been either ineffective or non-existent and had it not been for the gallantry, determination, dash and skilful use of fire-power on the part of Maj Brooks and his sqn, it is conceivable that this Bn's casualties and those of C Coy 1 C Scot R would have been much heavier and the capture of the beach-head greatly delayed.

During the advance inland both B and C Sqns, when asked for assistance in neutralizing enemy machine guns at Banville and Ste Croix-sur-Mer, brought everything they had to bear on to the task. Maj Stuart Duncan, commanding B Sqn and Maj D'Arcy Marks, commanding C Sqn, used their fire power with complete disregard for their own safety, unhesitatingly crossing suspected minefields and in the face of known anti-tank fire making possible the advance of D Coy through Banville and strongly supporting A Coy through the Ste Croix objective.

Time and again throughout D Day, without thought of their own safety or state of fatigue, these sqns of the 6 Cdn Armd Regt came to the assistance of this Bn. In paying high tribute to their gallantry, skill and cool daring it is regretted that the heat and speed of the action prevented recognition and consequent comment on the actions of troop commanders and individual crew commanders. It is stated, without hesitation, however, that no higher degree of courage or calculated daring could be displayed than that shown by every commander and sub-unit of this gallant Regt.

It is sincerely hoped that, in addition to this inadequate tribute, official recognition of the services rendered by the 6 Cdn Armd Regt is being given earnest consideration.

(JOHN MELDRUM) Lt-Col,
CC THE ROYAL WINNIPEG RIFLES

JMM/RKW

II
2 Cdn Army Tk. Bde.
I hearily agree with these sentiments.
H Foster, Brig.

Air photo of Courseulles taken late on D-Day. CFPU PL 144859

Lt Col F M Matheson, OC, Regina Rifles....

The two assaulting coys of Regina Rif touched down on Nan Green beach before Courseulles, 969858 to 984855. A Coy on the right was to assault the pillboxes from the mouth of the R Seulles to about half-way along the beach. On the left, B Coy was to land on the remainder of the beach. Both coys were slightly late and unfavourable weather conditions denied any effective sp whatsoever to A Coy ... (RMAS Centaurs had failed to appear and the DD tks in this area had been drowned.) Hits on the concrete fortress by hy projectiles had not cracked it. While B Coy met with little trouble, A on the other hand, found their first task a long and arduous one. They eventually executed a left flanking attack which succeeded in breaking through the defs.

For purposes of assault the town of Courseulles had been partitioned into blocks numbered 1 to 12, each to be cleared by designated coys. Careful study of enlarged aerial phs and maps showing the sites of enemy strong pts and made the ground itself easily recognizable. In fact, Lt Col Matheson said, nearly every foot of the town was known long before it was ever entered. At the same time, trg in street fighting had been carried out in anticipation of resistance in the town.

The strong pt engaged by A Coy was contained in Block 1. Further East B Coy assaulted Block 2, and having cleared it in good time, moved on to 3. Bn HQ now landed on the beach. Successful again in 3, B Coy proceeded to 4. A Coy was still held up at 1.

The res coys now commenced to come ashore. C Coy touched down without mishap and moved through the town to clear Block 8. But D Coy's craft were blown up in the water by mines and only 49 survivors reached land. The remnants reorganized within Courseulles and set out for Reviers, 9681, as planned.

C Coy next reported Block 8 clear and Bn HQ established itself there. C Coy then cleared in a short time Blocks 9, 10 and 11. A Coy now reported Block 1 in their hands, and were ordered to take on 5, 6 and 7 on the lock bank. Shortly afterwards B Coy had cleared 4 and was sent on to 12.

Now came a report from A Coy that they were being fired on from Block 1, only just mopped up. They had neglected to leave there a small force to prevent re-occupation and the enemy had swiftly returned to the SW corner of the strong pt by tunnels and trenches. It was therefore necessary to return to this corner and begin the disheartening work once again. Matters progressed so slowly that another tp of tks was assigned to them for assistance. Meanwhile, C Coy, having

finished with Block 11, set out for Reviers, following the remnants of D, whose leading elements had arrived there about 1100 hrs.

Comns between Bn HQ and A Coy now broke down and the 21C set out to find them. He returned with the report that they had now gone on to Block 5 and would remain in Courseulles to complete its clearance (Blocks 6 and 7).

Bn HQ followed C Coy to Reviers and established itself there about 1500 hrs. Lt Col Matheson pointed out here that exact reconstruction of time was impossible and refs to the hr of the day could only be vague. B Coy next arrived in Reviers, followed after an interval by A, and the bn rested there, awaiting bde orders to move on. Many PW had been taken there by surprise.

Lt Col Matheson was of the opinion that Courseulles contained more tps than had been expected from Int Reports. In any event about 80 Germans were taken in the town, and many more had been killed or had escaped South.

The bn's trg in street fighting stood them in good stead even though the clearing of Courseulles did not involve house-to-house battles (as is clear from the comparatively short time required to take it).

The sp of tks of B Sqn, 6 Cdn Armd Regt, was invaluable on the beach. That their work was not done without losses is shown by the fact that only ten tks were still operational when the bn reached Reviers.

The build up on "Nan Green" beach. Courseulles, D-Day.
PA 128791/Public Archives Canada.

Advance Inland D-Day

'C' Company of the North Shores was able to move through the western edge of St. Aubin and on to Tailleville shortly after ten o'clock. Accompanied by a troop of Fort Garries, they fought their way south, overcoming two gun positions and 'about 50 infantry'. By-passing Tailleville, the tanks took up position on the rising ground beyond the village, then turned to help the infantry. 'C' Company 'worked forward to the wall of the town. It soon became apparent that the defences were much stronger than reported. The position was well dug in and tunnelled. Persistent sniping was most annoying to the attackers'.

With one company still at work consolidating St. Aubin, the rest of the North Shores moved on to assist 'C' Company. Tailleville contained a battalion headquarters and a company of the 736 Grenadier Regiment. The air and naval bombardment had wrecked the village but the sheltered troops had ample time to recover before the Canadians reached them. It was late afternoon when the ruins were under control and even then sniping persisted well into the next day.

Part of the North Shore - Fort Garry force was ready to move on to the heavily fortified radar stations by mid-afternoon but both flanks were wide open and the fortress anti-tank guns ahead had a clear field of fire down the slope to Tailleville. The Commandos had still not overcome the enemy in Langrune and both Luc sur Mer and La Delivrande were untouched. Nor was help on the way. Crocker, the Corps Commander, ordered the 9th British Brigade to cancel its original plan of going straight down on the division's right flank 'to get Carpiquet' but instead to move left to support the 6th Airborne. This meant that the wide gap between the Canadians and British could not be closed on D-Day. The situation on the North Shore's right flank was not much better. At 1400 hours Brigadier Blackader signalled 'Sunray says to watch out next step because Chaudiere is not very far forward yet'. In fact the Regiment de Chaudiere had not left its first assembly position. A 'hidden 88 gun' had pinned the assault troops down at the southern edge of Bernieres.

Aboard the command ship HMS 'Hillary', General Rod Keller was desperately trying to make sense of the battle. For Keller the crucial decision was when and where to land the reserve brigade, the force which was to pass through the beachhead and rush for the divisional objective, the high ground around Carpiquet airport. The preferred plan was to land the 9th Brigade at Bernieres and St. Aubin and the scheduled timing was between H + 4 and H + 6 hours. The alternate plan was to pass the 9th through the Courseulles beaches. Hindsight would suggest that Keller made the wrong decision but the message log of 3rd Division headquarters indicates that his order to land the 9th Brigade on the eastern beachhead made sense in terms of the information available to him.

Before Keller's decision a steady stream of messages from 8th Brigade units had painted a very optimistic picture. As late as 1050 the Chaudieres were said to be 'making progress slowly' and, of course, the North Shores had reported 'proceeding according to plan'. Keller did not know that the Navy had closed Nan Red beach at St. Aubin forcing the entire Brigade to land at Bernieres. News from the 7th Brigade was sparse and the signal 'troops in Banville and Ste. Croix', while timed at 1041, was logged after 1050 when the landing order was issued. It was not until 1215 that the 8th Brigade finally admitted 'Progress slow after Yew, (the road inland from the beach). Trying to engage 88 battery. Naval support requested'.

The reserve brigade was, therefore, committed to land on a narrow beach whose exits were already packed with troops of the 8th Brigade. No one who was at Bernieres that day will ever forget the confusion as vehicles and men milled about. A massive traffic jam had developed in the narrow streets of the village as no one could move forward. Drivers took the opportunity to de-waterproof their vehicles which further immobilized the procession. 'Into this mess the 9th Brigade began landing ... the roads were plugged with zealous soldiers impatient to get on. Fortunately, the Germans did not shell the town'. Fortunate indeed. Ross Munroe, the Canadian Press correspondent, who had been at the Dieppe and Sicily landings, took one look and got as far away as he could! At 1245 Keller went ashore to discover that no one was moving

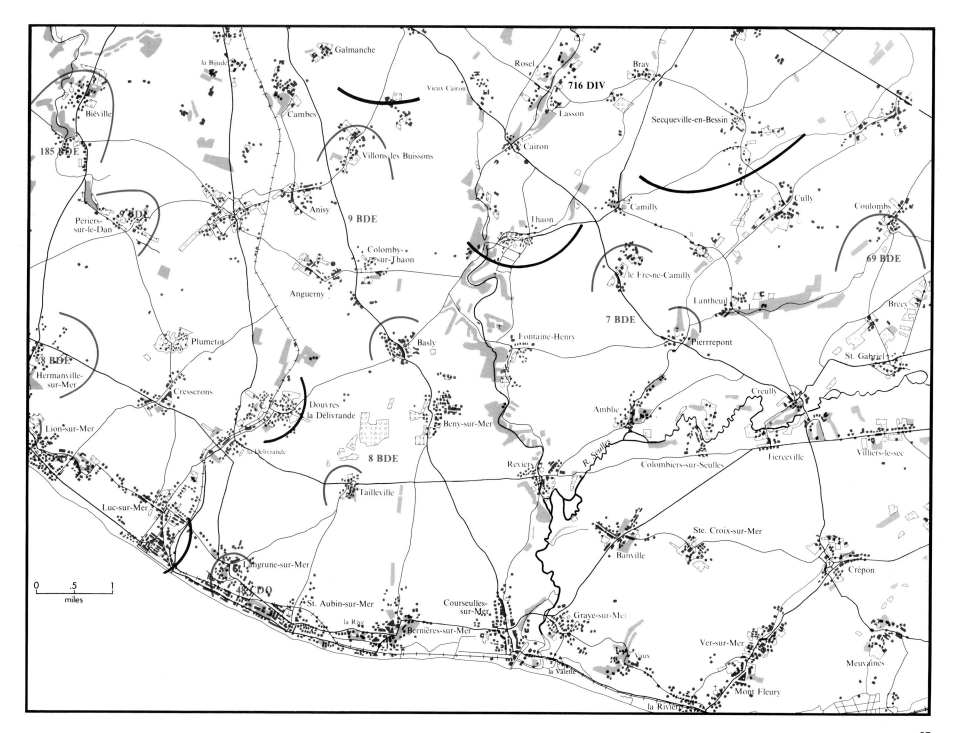

la Bijude

Galmanche

Rosel

Bray

716 DIV

Biéville

Cambes

Vieux Cairon

Lasson

Secqueville-en-Bessin

185 BDE

Villons-les-Buissons

Cairon

Anisy

9 BDE

Camilly

Cully

Périers-sur-le-Dan

BDE

Thaon

Coulombs

Colomby-sur-Thaon

le Fresne-Camilly

69 BDE

Anguerny

Lantheuil

Brécy

7 BDE

Plumetot

Basly

Fontaine-Henry

Pierrepont

8 BDE

Hermanville-sur-Mer

St. Gabriel

Cresserons

Douvres la Délivrande

Creully

Lion-sur-Mer

Amblie

Beny-sur-Mer

la Délivrande

8 BDE

Reviers

Colombiers-sur-Seulles

Tierceville

Villiers-le-sec

R. Seulles

Taillevelle

Luc-sur-Mer

Ste. Croix-sur-Mer

Langrune-sur-Mer

Banville

Crépon

48 DO

St. Aubin-sur-Mer

Courseulles-sur-Mer

la Rive

Graye-sur-Mer

Bernières-sur-Mer

Ver-sur-Mer

Vaux

Meuvaines

la Valette

Mont Fleury

la Rivière

0   .5   1
miles

57

forward. Blackader, Cunningham and their officers were desperately trying to sort out the situation as Keller charged furiously into the confusion, demanding action. It was not until early afternoon that the QOR's and Chaudieres were able to move cautiously forward and by 1430, Beny Sur Mer still required 'mopping up'. By early evening the 9th Brigade had been able to get its vanguard, the North Nova Scotias, clear of the traffic and on the road to Carpiquet but, by 2000 hours, when the halt order was issued, the North Novas had just reached Villons les Buissons and the rest of the brigade was strung out behind on the road from Beny.

Under British double daylight summer time it was far from dark at 2000 hours, but it had been a long, dangerous, exhausting and frustrating day. Keller, like all the Allied generals, was obsessed with the threat, of a Panzer counter-attack. Intelligence had estimated that both 21st and 12th SS Panzer divisions could intervene in the battle by late afternoon and news of 21st Panzer's attack on 3rd British Division had reached Canadian headquarters. It was time to dig in and secure the beachhead.

The 7th Brigade was not slowed down by a single massive traffic jam, but there was great difficulty in getting the beach exits open and keeping them that way. German resistance inland from Courseulles has often been described as weak and scattered, but this view is not shared by all of the soldiers who were there. The Royal Winnipeg Rifles encountered strong opposition at Ste. Croix sur Mer and were in danger of being pushed back. The Canadian Scottish, as the reserve battalion, were supposed to stay out of this fight so they could push through as the Brigade's vanguard. Instead they were drawn into the struggle for Ste. Croix and the momentum of the Brigade's advance was seriously checked.

The Reginas moved inland from Courseulles and were at Reviers by midday after some sharp encounters with anti-tank guns. They regrouped and tried to recover from the trauma of the assault. Ordered forward at 1430 they encountered heavy mortar fire and at 1700 hours were just 1000 yards south of Reviers, reporting 'progress slow'. The Winnipegs made it to Colombiers by 1315 and reported the occupation of Tierceville at 1500 hours. Shortly before, one company of the Winnipegs had made contact with the Green Howards of the British 50th Division, the first link up between the beaches on D-Day.

The Canadian Scottish disentangled from Ste. Croix and during the course of the afternoon got astride the main Arromanches-Caen highway. Progress was slow with much time spent on overcoming scattered mortar and machine gun positions and flushing out German stragglers. An artillery position near Camilly was overcome at 1715 hours and the village occupied shortly thereafter. By then the Reginas had pushed through Thaon and their commanding officer, Lt. Col. Matheson, met up with the Scottish in Camilly. There was not much resistance left in front of the 7th Brigade but it was not grouped for an organized push forward. One troop of First Hussar tanks which had fought with the Winnipegs, raced on towards the objective and made it all the way to Secqueville-en-Bessin without encountering serious opposition. Finding themselves isolated without infantry or anti-tank support they retraced their steps. The Canadian Scottish was ordered to 'not proceed further' at 2033 and they eventually withdrew their vanguard to La Fresne-Camilly. How Keller must have longed to have had the 9th Brigade in position to exploit the situation of the 7th Brigade front!

The traffic jam at Bernieres as the 9th Brigade lands. CFPU PL 144862/3.

59

Brigadier Blackader.....

By 1025 SP (self-propelled) artillery, tanks and Chauds were linked up. All had gone per plan thus far. The first three SP's of 14th Field Regiment had just pulled off to a field at the right of the road and the detachments were preparing a gun position when a hidden 88 gun fired on them, hitting all three in a matter of less than a minute. They burst into flames and the huge quantity of ammunition on them (in addition to 105's this included extra ammunition and mines) commenced to explode. The detonations lasted over an hour and made this area exceedingly dangerous. As a result of this incident the tanks were loath to leave cover and advance up the grassy field.

It was then decided to move the infantry forward, along the road. But they came under MG crossfire. It was impossible to locate either gun or MGs in the long grass and it therefore became necessary to delay the advance until scouting or recce parties could pinpoint the opposition so that it could be dealt with. This was finally achieved by siting the artillery in another section of Bernieres and directing their fire on the presumed location. By this means and under cover of MG fire by the Cameron Highlanders of Ottawa our infantry was able to infiltrate up the road.

This delay of approximately two hours was very costly because it slowed down the forward move of 9th Brigade. Eventually the Brigade got underway and proceeded to its other tasks.

General "Rod" Keller comes ashore D-Day. PA 115544/Public Archives Canada.

The Rhino Ferry by O. N.
Fisher. (12468)

The German Reaction

'*Bercent mon coeur d'une longeur monotone*', misquoting the second part of Verlaine's poem, the BBC at about 2115 hours on the evening of June 5th called on Ventriliquist, a section of the French Resistance, to begin full stage railway sabotage in an area south of Orleans. The invasion would follow within forty-eight hours. German intelligence was aware of the meaning of this message, but the use made of this knowledge was a harbinger for the whole conduct of the German campaign in Normandy.

Lt. Colonel Meyer, the intelligence officer of the 15th Army, immediately informed his Commander-in-Chief, General von Salmuth, who alerted all his subordinate units, so that within the hour all units of the 15th Army were standing at Alert II, the highest state of readiness for the German military in France. The intelligence officer at Rommel's headquarters, Col. Staubwasser, was also informed. Rommel had left for Germany the previous morning (Sunday, June 4th) to celebrate his wife's birthday and to try and see Hitler who was in Obersalzburg. Lt. General Speidel, Rommel's Chief of Staff was the senior officer in charge during his absence and Staubwasser interrupted his dinner party in order to relay the message. He was told to seek the advice of Rundstedt's headquarters. According to Staubwasser's account, a staff officer there shrugged the matter off as another false alarm and told him that there was no reason to institute an Alert II. By midnight, therefore, the 15th Army was fully alerted, while its neighbour, the 7th Army, where the Allies would land, was not informed.

Major Hayn, the intelligence officer of the 84th Army Corps, the subordinate unit of the 7th Army which lay directly in the path of the Allied invasion forces, had received no warning. He was waiting for the cathedral tower in St. Lo to strike midnight, so that he could take a bottle of Chablis into the command bunker to celebrate the birthday of General Marcks, Commander in Chief of the 84th Corps who would be 53 years old on June 6th. There would be no other occasion to do so as all the commanding officers of the 7th Army had been called to Rennes for a map exercise the next morning. The celebration was very short, for the one-legged commander was busily preparing for the war game.

A few minutes past one, however, a number of divisional commands began to report the arrival of the Allied parachute troops and by 0200 hours it was fairly clear that a large operation was in progress. The divisions of the 7th Army were quickly placed on full alert and by 0235 hours the situation was serious enough to release the 91st Division, of the 7th Army reserve in the neighbourhood of the US airdrop. As the reports of Allied parachute and glider landings mounted and air activity increased along coastal sectors, the local German commands became increasingly convinced that they were facing an invasion. Moreover by 0300 hours German time those commands were also aware that there were large numbers of ships standing off the coast, so that by 0345 hours, the Chief of Staff of the 7th Army summarized the situation to Rommel's headquarters as a major action with two main centres - one, the mouth of the Orne river, and the other, near St. Mere Eglise. He added that landing craft were approaching the coast. While Rommel's headquarters remained sceptical, it did alert the 21st Panzer Division which hardly needed alerting since its forward elements had been in action with the British Airborne troops for some hours.

The need to eliminate the airborne troops now seems to have become the main preoccupation and at 0520 General Feuchtinger, the commander of the 21st Panzer Division, informed the 7th Army that he would launch attacks on both sides of the Orne, the main effort being concentrated on the east side of the river.

Rundstedt's headquarters, although doubtful that this was the main invasion, took somewhat more far-reaching steps. Before 0500 hours it ordered the 12th SS Panzer Division to move to Lisieux, behind the 711th Inf. Div. east of the Orne and the Panzer Lehr Division to move forward towards the coast in readiness for immediate commitment. OKW countermanded these orders at 1000 hours; although it allowed the 12th SS to continue its movement, it stopped any move by Panzer Lehr and forbade the commitment of either division without express permission from the Supreme Command. It was necessary to clarify the situation before any major commitment could be allowed.

During the course of the morning both the 84th Corps and the 7th Army began to appreciate the gravity of the situation. The Allies had come ashore in at least five areas and had made deep penetrations west of the Orne river where the situation was rapidly becoming critical. The 21st Panzer Division was formally attached to the 84th Corps at 0700 hours, its infantry regiments had been fighting for some time to try to win back the bridges at Ranville-Benouville, but had not succeeded. At 1035 General Marcks ordered the armoured units to concentrate on the west side of the Orne river, and this change in direction slowed down the approach of the armour. Marcks himself drove to the command post of the 192nd Panzer Regiment of the Division in the early afternoon and saw it launch the only major counterattack of the day. Parts of it briefly broke through to the coast but by 2100 hours it had been stopped and, with no prospect of reinforcement, the regiment was forced to fight its way back to a line just north of Caen. It had lost 25% of its armour.

From the areas of the US landings there was more optimistic news with no deep penetrations reported, but in that sector, the Germans were plagued by rumours that another airborne assault had occurred in the area Constance-Lessay. Since they were aware that the Allies had at their disposal more than the three airborne divisions already identified, and presumed that one of the prime objectives was the cutting of the Cotentin peninsula, these reported landings proved a source of considerable unease and led General Marcks to order the Corps reserve (915th Inf. Regt. of the 352nd Inf. Div.) to the area. As there were no landings, it was a case of reinforcements spending some vital hours moving in the wrong direction. By late afternoon, 1800 hours, the situation at the US beaches had deteriorated sufficiently for the 7th Army to release some of its reserves to the St. Mere Eglise-Carentan-Madelaine sectors for a counter-attack.

During the night of the 6th and in the early hours of Wednesday morning Rommel and Dollman (Commander in Chief of the 7th Army) reached the conclusion that the western part of the front would need more substantial reinforcements. The II Parachute Corps was ordered to

Field Marshall von Rundstedt.

63

the battle-front from the Brittany peninsula. It was to bring with it from Brittany, the 3rd Parachute Division and the 77th Inf. Division and would have the 17th Panzer Grenadier Division attached as soon as it could arrive from south of the Loire river. It had been released from OKW reserve. The Combat Groups of the 265th, 275th Infantry Divisions stationed along the Brittany coast were also ordered to Normandy and the 346th Infantry Division began crossing the Seine river to reinforce the 711th Infantry Division. The race to reinforce the troops fighting in the bridgehead area had begun.

None of these improvised movements touched on the essential issue of the use of armoured divisions. The 7th Army had repeatedly pressed Rommel's headquarters to obtain release of 12 SS and Panzer Lehr Divisions from OKW reserve and finally at 1505 hours General Speidel was able to inform the 7th Army that these two divisions together with 21st Panzer Division would be grouped together under 1st Panzer Corps and ordered to launch a coordinated counter-attack at the Anglo-Canadian Bridgehead on June 7th. This was in line with Rommel's doctrine that rapid commitment of the armoured divisions was necessary to prevent the Allies from consolidating their position. But Rommel's theory had assumed that the armour would be in position and that the Atlantic Wall was capable of holding up the Allied advance. In fact the British-Canadian assault forces had penetrated well beyond the coastal strong points and had decimated the regiments defending them. The 21st Panzer Division was already deeply committed to a bitter holding action with the British 3rd Division and could not be withdrawn. Between Caen and Bayeux the Germans had only remnants of the two infantry regiments to counter the advance of 3rd Canadian and 50th British Division. How could the two reserve Panzer Divisions, arriving in bits and pieces, possibly launch a 'coordinated counter-attack'?

The 12th SS had been moving forward towards the front since dawn on D-Day, but air attacks, blocked roads and the sheer complexity of moving 20,000 men and their vehicles meant that the division was strung out on the roads to the east of Caen. The division's vanguard, the 25th

Panzer Grenadier Regiment, had reached Lisieux when it was ordered to subordinate itself, first to 84 Corps, then to 1st SS Panzer Corps for the coordinated attack. The direction of the columns had to be changed to reach the new assembly area west of Caen since the Allied airborne troops blocked the routes across the Orne to the north of the city.

When the commander of the 25th Panzer Grenadier Regiment, Kurt Meyer, established his headquarters in the Ardennes Abbey on the morning of June 7th he discovered that the Canadian 9th Brigade was already moving across his left flank to Carpiquet airport. He was informed that the Luftwaffe ground troops had abandoned the airport defences and he knew the rest of the division, which was to cover the left flank as far as Tilly sur Seulles, would not arrive for many hours. Despite his orders to prepare for a coordinated counter-attack the Canadians had left him with no real choice. If he waited his whole position would be outflanked.

Meyer ordered his regiment to attack the exposed flank of the Canadians hoping that 21st Panzer Division would also launch an assault. The Canadians were taken by surprise and struck with great force. They were expelled from Authie and Buron after taking heavy losses in men and tanks. There was no attack by 21st Panzer Division and Meyer had to cancel a push north to Ainsy. He then had to withdraw from Buron when the guns of a British cruiser intervened in the battle. Sharp though it was, the attack of a single regiment could hardly pose a threat to the Allied position.

The whole process was repeated the next day when the 26th Panzer Grenadier Regiment of the 12th SS arrived to find that the Canadian 7th Brigade had reached the Caen-Bayeux road and were digging in. German battle doctrine, reinforced by Rommel's specific instructions, led the regiment to make repeated frontal assaults on the 7th Brigade and though some ground was gained initially, it was quickly lost when the Canadians put in a fierce counter-attack. The 26th Regiment found itself committed to a defensive role.

The Ardennes Abbey where Kurt Meyer watched the approach of the 9th Brigade. Photographed in 1946. DND PMR 82-082.

Elements of Panzer Lehr Division also began arriving on the 8th to take over the left flank of 12th SS opposite British 50th Division. One of its regiments was soon embroiled in a battle with British troops in the Bronay area. 'Sepp' Dietrich, the commander of I Panzer Corps, ordered the rest of Panzer Lehr to advance towards Bayeux along the Tilly sur Seulles highway. That night, June 8th-9th, General Geyr von Schweppenburg, Commander-in-Chief of Panzer Group West overruled Dietrich and tried to regroup the three Panzer Divisions for a united effort on the 11th or 12th. This plan was postponed on the 10th because of strong pressure from the Canadians. A few minutes later the headquarters of Panzer Group West, which had been pinpointed by Ultra, was destroyed by RAF Typhoons. Nearly all of von Schweppenburg's staff was killed and its communication equipment destroyed. 'Sepp' Dietrich's I SS Panzer Corps was now placed in charge of the scheme but continued Allied pressure, including the Canadian attack on Le Mensil Patry, forced the Germans to use all available troops to prevent a breakthrough.

At OB West Rundstedt was more concerned with the gap between Panzer Lehr and what was left of the 352nd Division. He had ordered 2nd SS Panzer Division (from Tours) and 2nd Panzer Division (from Amiens) into that area but they could not begin to arrive before the 12th of June. In the meantime he hoped that the vanguard of II Parachute Corps would be able to seal off the 'Caumont Gap'. Rommel thought he saw an even more critical situation developing from the American threat to Cherbourg and he diverted troops to that area. This left the 'Caumont Gap' covered by one Recce. unit of the 17th SS, quite alone in the face of two US infantry divisions and the right flank Brigade of British 50th Division.

The Allies attempted to exploit this weakness by thrusting 7th British Armoured Division down the road to Villers Bocage on June 12th and 13th. The German's only available armour reserve, a company of Tiger tanks was committed and the 7th Armour stopped, allowing reinforcements to arrive and the line to be stabilized.

Hitler intervened in the battle on the 12th with the demand that the bridgehead be destroyed sector by sector beginning with the area east of the Orne. Given the German distribution of troops this edict might have been regarded as comic relief but the German Generals hastened to obey. The British troops in the Orne bridgehead, the 6th Airborne and the 51st Highland Division blunted these attacks which were never strong enough to seriously threaten the Allied lines. There were too many headquarters directing too few divisions for the Germans to accomplish anything except the establishment of a defensive line. Now it was a question of which side could build up enough reserves to alter the balance.

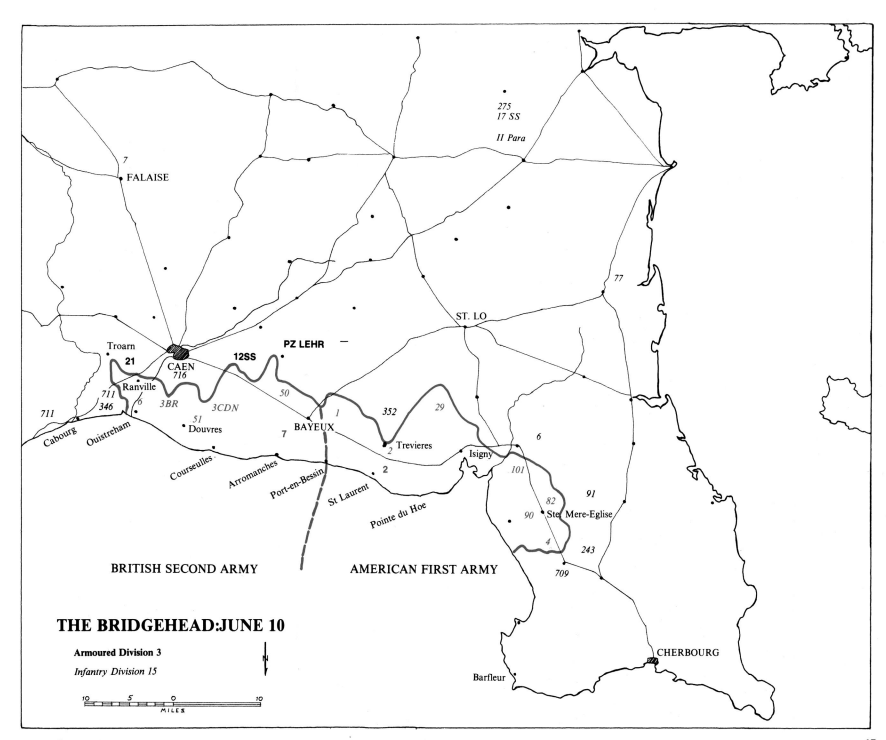

THE BRIDGEHEAD:JUNE 10

7 FALAISE

275
17 SS

II Para

77

ST. LO

Troarn

21

Ranville

CAEN
716

12SS

PZ LEHR

711
346

711

6

3BR

3CDN

50

1

352

29

6

Cabourg

Ouistreham

51
Douvres

7

BAYEUX

2

101

91

Courseulles

Arromanches

Port-en-Bessin

St Laurent

2

Trevieres

Isigny

82

90

Ste Mere-Eglise

Pointe du Hoe

4

243

BRITISH SECOND ARMY

AMERICAN FIRST ARMY

709

Armoured Division 3

Infantry Division 15

N

CHERBOURG

Barfleur

10 5 0 10
MILES

The 9th Brigade Advance

For most officers and men, the night of June 6th-7th provided little chance for sleep. There was no organized counter-attack but small groups of the enemy probed or stumbled into the scattered Canadian battalions. The Chaudieres had a particularly hot fire-fight with some German half-tracks. Brigade and Divisional staff officers worked through the night trying to sort out a very confused situation. For the 8th Brigade the task was clear enough. The North Shores would have another 'go' at the radar station and the other battalions would mop up. The 7th would continue its advance, two battalions up, along the planned axis.

The 9th Brigade was in a more difficult position. It would move on to Carpiquet hoping that a British Brigade would be able to catch up along its left flank at least as far as St. Contest. Brigadier Cunningham held his Orders Group at 0500. A composite battle group of North Novas, Sherbrooke tanks, M10's and medium machine guns, (Cameron Highlanders of Ottawa) would advance to Buron, Authie, Francqueville and Carpiquet. Once they moved forward however, they would be out of artillery range until the SP's of the 14th Field Regiment could be leap-frogged forward. Unfortunately, the artillery would have to move along the same road that the Glengarries and HLI would use to close up with their lead battalion. It was hoped that naval support would be available throughout the day.

At first everything went according to plan. Les Buissons was cleared after a pincer attack took out an anti-tank gun and 16 barrelled mortar. A second anti-tank gun was destroyed by tank fire on the road to Buron. At 1150 Buron was occupied although pockets of Germans were hidden in the area. 'C' Company in the lead with 'A' and 'B' on its flanks, moved on to Authie leaving 'D' Company to deal with holdouts. By 1230 Authie was reached and the light reconnaissance tanks of the Sherbrookes went on to Francqueville. Then it started. Artillery and mortar fire from the higher ground to the left began to blast the area. One squadron of the Sherbrookes tried to put in an attack against St. Contest but were not strong enough to push through. 'C' Company dug in around Authie waiting for artillery support.

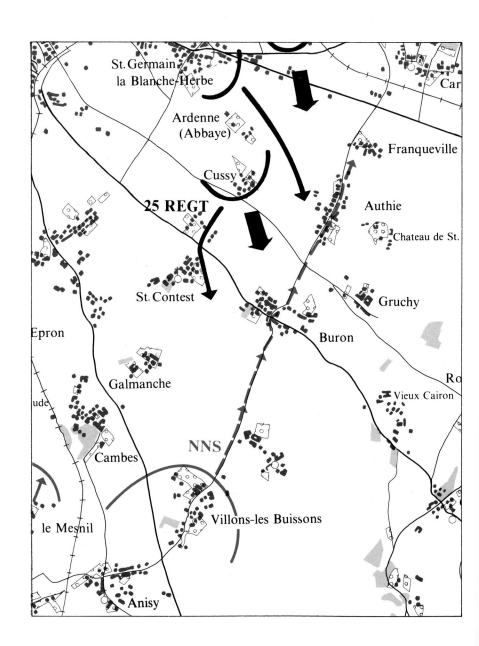

Back along the road to Beny the chaos of D-Day was returning. The Glengarries had been very slow in getting started and the road was soon choked with transport. The 14th Field Regiment was in the midst of its move forward and could offer no support to the North Novas. The young Royal Navy officer attached to the 9th had lost wireless contact with the assigned Cruiser and 'was actually in tears at his failure to provide support'.

'C' Company in Authie could not be reinforced because the road between Buron and their position was under heavy direct fire. The North Novas had run into a regiment of the 12th SS Panzer Division which was holding a defensive position northwest of Caen until the rest of the division arrived. Colonel Kurt Meyer, in command of 25th SS Panzer Grenadier Regiment, had watched the approach of the North Novas from the tower of the Ardenne Abbey and decided to counter-attack with two battalions supported by tanks. The North Novas in Authie were overrun after a vicious close quarters battle. Buron was attacked and a fierce tank battle raged around the village. Buron was lost just as contact was re-established with the Navy, (two wireless sets salvaged from tanks were used). With support from the big guns Buron was recaptured and further German attacks broken up but enemy artillery continued to pound the village and Cunningham brought the remaining men of the North Novas and Sherbrookes back to Les Buissons where the other battalions were preparing a 'fortress' position. The vanguard of the 9th Brigade had been decimated; 110 men were killed, 192 wounded and 120 taken prisoner. Twenty-one tanks had been knocked out. Losses equalled more than forty percent of all Canadian casualties on D-Day!

The day's events on the road to Carpiquet seem at first sight to suggest that if Rommel had had his way and the Panzer Divisions had been stationed close to the beaches, the story of D Day would have been very different. It is however, much more relevant to point out that any advance along a single axis, without artillery support and with an open flank is an invitation to disaster. Crocker, the Commander of 1st British Corps, and Keller based their plans for June 7th on the assumption that 3rd British Division could make rapid progress and parallel the Canadian advance; in the event the 185th Brigade was stopped at Lebisey Woods and the 9th Brigade was repulsed at Cambes late in the day. Cunningham has been criticized for his handling of the battle because the artillery was out of range most of the day and his two other battalions were too far back to assist the North Novas. This situation was a legacy of the D-Day confusion on this front. The best plan for June 7th was to take the time to organize a full Brigade Group advance with close artillery support and careful reconnaissance of the flanks. But on the morning of June 7th no one was prepared to wait until such an advance could be organized. The caution of D-Day had given way to a new and quite unwarranted optimism.

The same optimism had sent the 7th Brigade charging forward to their D-Day objective. Fortunately, there was no Panzer Regiment in front of them and the lead companies of the Reginas and Winnipegs were at 'OAK' by late morning. There they dug in with the Winnipegs at Putot and the Reginas at Bretteville, and Norrey. The 7th Brigade was out in front of all other Allied troops with both flanks exposed.

North Nova Scotia Highlanders

June 7, 1944.

At 0740 hours the Battalion again moved off in the same order, changing our axis of advance through Villons-les-Buissons along the main road to Carpiquet. By 0930 hours the village of Les Buissons was cleared and the command post moved up to that point. After some heavy mortar fire from St. Contest, the vanguard captured Buron and reported 'Ale' at 1150 hours. At 1230 hours the leading elements of the vanguard who had reached Authie reported 'Danube' and were closely followed on the right by 'A' company on 'A' squadron of tanks. Shortly after this the stuarts of 27 Canadian Armoured Regiment reported 'Eve' (Frankville). The vanguard reached Authie and encountered three machine gun posts and hectic fighting took place. The vanguard commander reported mortar and shell fire from both flanks and the front, and asked for a troop of tanks and some artillery to take it on. The Forward Observation Officer then reported that artillery was out of range and it would be some time before it could be moved up.

The only fire available was a cruiser, which the Naval Forward Observation Officer said could engage St. Contest for twenty minutes. This fire would have wiped St. Contest out, but faulty communications made it impossible to obtain it in time. In the meantime the troop of tanks had reached the vanguard and all were hit by 88 millimetres. The vanguard was then ordered to dig in and form a firm base. In the Commanding Officer's opinion it was impossible to go on. There was no one within miles of us on either flank or in the rear, so the flanking companies were ordered to close up on 'C' company and form a fortress. The vanguard commander wanted to come back to high ground in the rear of Authie. This permission was granted, and 'A' company who had not yet arrived, dug in on the right, just North of Authie. 'B' company were ordered up to dig in on their left and the rest of the battalion to bring up the rear. While this was in progress the vanguard was heavily attacked from the direction of St. Contest - Cussy by at least nine tanks and about two companies of infantry. It was too late for the vanguard to withdraw to the battalion position so they decided to fight it out in front of Authie. Captain FLC. Fraser, who was with the leading elements, took command of the situation and hastily organized the defence, taking the Brownings from three knocked out tanks and a machine gun from the platoon commander's carrier of the Cameron Highlanders of Ottawa, who had become a casualty. Nothing further was heard from this small formation and no one escaped to tell the story of their gallant action. At about the same time German armour struck past Authie and it could be seen a major counter-attack was being launched. All available tanks from 'A' and 'B' squadrons manouvered from hull-down positions South of Buron and

Instructions regarding
preparation of War
Diaries; are contained in
F.S. Regs. Vol. 1.

WAR DIARY

Original, duplicate and
triplicate to be forward-
ed to O. i/c 2nd
Echelon for disposal.

North Nova Scotia Highlanders

June 7, 1944. (continued)

as enemy armour broke through a great tank battle took place. At 1630 hours it was found that it was impossible for the battalion to push forward to Authie and Major Learment was ordered by the Commanding Officer to bring the forward troops back and form a fortress just on the outskirts South of Buron.

'A' company were surrounded by tanks and infantry and unable to withdraw to the battalion fortress. Shortly after this the position South of Buron came under very heavy shell fire and mortar fire and when armour broke around our flanks the position became untenable. As there was no field of fire on the flanks the remainder of the battalion was facing another encircling movement had they remained in their positions. Major Learment who was then in command of the two forward companies with Captain Wilson then in command of the remnants of 'B' company were ordered to withdraw to the previously dug slit trenches, in rear of 'D' company and the battalion went to ground and prepared to hold on to the last. As the tanks came round the flank the remaining tanks of the 27 Canadian Armoured Regiment and the Self Propelled guns of the Anti-Tank opened up from the woods of Les Buissons and also small arms fire from machine guns and brownings over the heads of our troops to the North fringe of Buron. The enemy then engaged our fire from Buron with 75,88s mortars and everything they had. Under this fire enemy infantry advanced and penetrated the forward slit trenches of 'D' company. It was impossible to stop them as they had to remain in their trenches to avoid our overhead fire and also the enemies. They had no field of fire due to the high grain. Machine gun fire and grenades were fired into the slits and 10 platoon and 16 platoon having run out of ammunition were forced to surrender and were rounded up.

Under our heavy Artillery fire which followed the captors went to ground and in the moment afforded by this break two sections of 16 platoon escaped and returned to their company. About this time one of 'D' company men reported to Battalion Headquarters that the forward positions were overrun and they were out of communication with everybody and that support was needed immediately. A fast counter-attack was immediately ordered by the Commanding Officer. Fierce fighting followed, and under a heavy artillery concentration on the forward position of 'D' company quickly laid on by our Forward Observation Officer we counter-attacked with the 12 remaining tanks which moved out under cover of the barrage. Artillery fire got the enemy in our forward position and with the help of the tanks they were driven out of Buron to Authie. Many casualties were inflicted by the tanks' guns and in some instances the enemy being so numerous they were run over by them.

North Nova Scotia Highlanders

June 7, 1944. (continued)	*The town of Buron was re-captured, but by this time we could only account for part of 'D' company and the remnants of 'B' and 'C' companies, which was not sufficient strength, and as it was getting dark it was impossible to consolidate there and hold the position overnight. In view of this, permission was asked of the Brigadier to withdraw to the high ground in the woods at Les Buissons with the Stormont Dundas and Glengarry Highlanders and the remainder of the 27 Canadian Armoured Regiment. Permission was granted and the remnants of 'D'. 'A', 'B', 'C' and Support Companies were withdrawn into the fortress. No counter-attack came in that night and the battalion prepared to go back and occupy the town next morning, but higher authority called this off and the remainder of the Brigade was brought up on our right to occupy the town of Les Buissons.*
	Casualties: Killed - Captain H. G. Longley and 10 Other Ranks; wounded - Major J. W. Douglas, Captain D. L. Clarke, Lieutenant H. E. Murphy and 27 Other Ranks; Missing - Major J. D. Learment, Major L. M. Rhodenizer, Captain F. C. Fraser, Captain J. A. Trainor, Lieutenant S. F. Campbell, Lieutenant J. L. Fairweather, Lieutenant J. H. Langley, Lieutenant G. A. P. Smith, Lieutenant J. M. Veness and 195 Other Ranks.

A Sherman tank of the 2nd Canadian Armoured Brigade with a 75 mm gun. The standard Sherman was no match for the German tanks but the Canadians and British usually had one Sherman "Firefly" equipped with the highly effective 17 pounder British anti-tank gun in each four tank troop. PA 129034/Public Archives Canada.

Attack on the 7th Brigade

Brigadier Harry Foster's 'Western' Brigade moved to positions astride the Caen-Bayeux highway in the early afternoon of the 7th. The Royal Winnipeg Rifles occupied Putot-en-Bessin with three companies forming a perimeter defence and a fourth in reserve. A flank guard was stationed north of Bronay to maintain contact with the Green Howards of the 50th Division. As night fell a German probing attack was beaten off and reinforcements arriving from the beachhead were hastily assigned to the weakest companies.

The Regina Rifles had set up a defensive position based on Bretteville l'Orqueilleuse with 'C' Company isolated across the railway line at Norrey-en-Bessin. The Canadian Scottish were held in reserve at Sequeville but when Foster learned of the fate of the 9th Brigade he detached one of its companies together with a squadron of First Hussars, and a troop of M 10s from the 3rd Anti-Tank Regiment, to cover the long exposed flank of the 7th Brigade. The self-propelled guns of the 12th and 13th Field Regiments were posted to provide all-round fire support. The medium machine guns and mortars of the Cameron Highlanders of Ottawa were carefully placed to counter any attack. The 7th Brigade had done its best to prepare an all-around defence but the lightly guarded left flank was a constant source of worry to Brigade headquarters.

Fortunately the 26th Panzer Grenadier Regiment arrived from the south, set up headquarters at Cheux and deployed its three battalions directly in front of the main Canadian positions. Shortly after dawn the first attacks began on Putot and Norrey; it was the beginning of a long bloody day. Two of the three enemy battalions were committed to Putot-Bronay section and by mid-afternoon three companies of the Winnipegs were cut off. The left wing of the German advance was checked by the arrival of the vanguard of the British 8th Armoured Brigade. Foster decided to commit his reserve battalion.

The Canadian Scottish, including the company defending the right flank, were hastily assembled, linked up with elements of he First Hussars and told to take the village. The two artillery field regiments laid down a creeping barrage and the Scottish followed close behind. After two hours of fierce fighting Putot was recaptured. But the battle was far from over. The 25th Panzer Grenadier Regiment and the division's Panther tank battalion had mounted an attack along the main highway with the intention of breaking through to Bayeux.

Kurt Meyer's decision to thrust his forces directly along the main highway was a critical mistake. There were no Canadian reserves and only a thin screen of anti-tank guns covered the entire left flank. As if to compound this strategic error, the 12th SS attacked Bretteville without having reduced the garrison at Norrey and they had to split their forces when they came under flank fire. Foster's decision to allow the stubborn 'Johns' of 'C' Company to stay in Norrey paid handsome dividends. Even so the battle of Bretteville raged all night in the streets of the village. At dawn the 12th SS withdrew having suffered heavy losses. The 7th Brigade had won a crucial defensive victory.

The cost of victory was high. The Royal Winnipeg Rifles had been devastated, taking 256 casualties including 105 dead. Many of the dead had been taken prisoner and then executed. The Canadian Scottish lost 125 men, 45 of them killed in action. The Regina's losses were thankfully smaller.

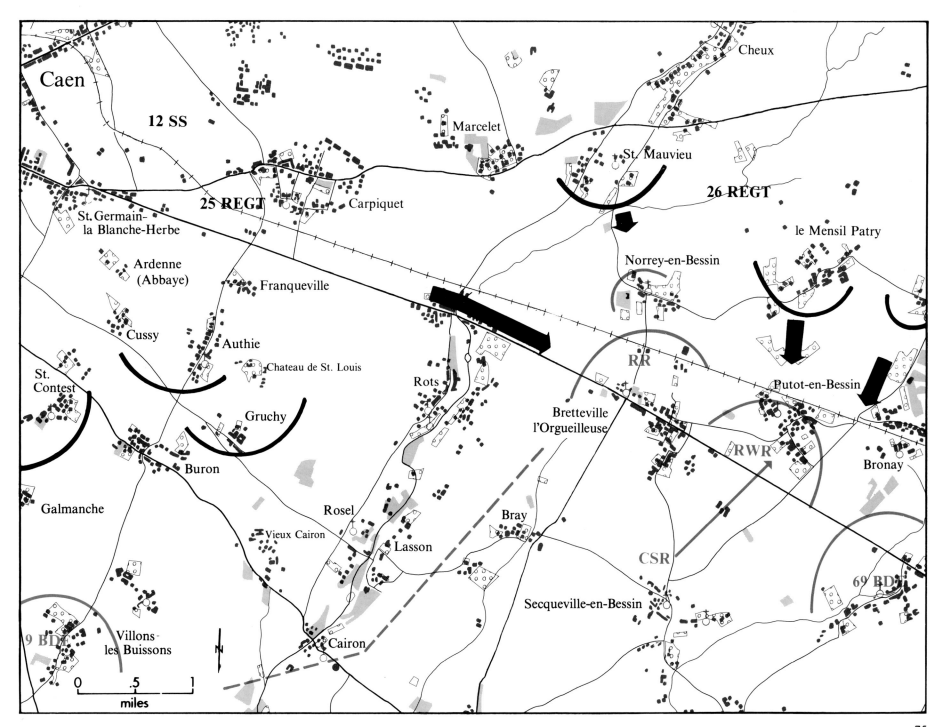

Caen

12 SS

25 REGT

St. Germain-
la Blanche-Herbe

Ardenne
(Abbaye)

Cussy

St.
Contest

Franqueville

Authie

Chateau de St. Louis

Gruchy

Buron

Galmanche

Vieux Cairon

Rosel

Lasson

Villons-
les Buissons

Cairon

Bray

Rots

Carpiquet

Marcelet

Cheux

St. Mauvieu

26 REGT

le Mensil Patry

Norrey-en-Bessin

RR

Bretteville
l'Orgueilleuse

Putot-en-Bessin

RWR

Bronay

CSR

Secqueville-en-Bessin

69 BD

9 BD

0   .5   1

miles

75

A Jeep ambulance of the Royal Canadian Army Medical Corps evacuating wounded.
PA 129031/Public Archives Canada.

Instructions regarding
preparation of War
Diaries; are contained in
F.S. Regs. Vol. 1.

WAR DIARY

Original, duplicate and
triplicate to be forward-
ed to O. i/c 2nd
Echelon for disposal.

Royal Winnipeg Rifles

Putot-en-Bessin
June 8, 1944.

During the night enemy machine guns had fired from posns South of the rly, hoping to draw our fire and pin point our posns. At 0400 hrs enemy tks were heard across the rly at 894720. As it became lighter, enemy tks, supported by inf attempted to cross the railway bridge in front of A Coy. The whole Bn area was subjected to enemy arty and mortar fire during this attack. This attack was repulsed by fire from A Coy assisted by one pl of MMGs, Cameron Highlanders of Ottawa, which were covering the rly br. Cpl Naylor's det of the A tk pl knocked out one PZKW Mark III tk, and one enemy armd car. During the early morning snipers came to life in the buildings throughout the town and made it increasingly difficult to move in the whole Bn area. At 1200 hrs more enemy had infiltrated into the town around our posns and there was direct enemy machine gun, mortar and arty fire on our LMG posts and individuals in slit trenches. It was now impossible to get amn to the coys, even with a Bren carrier. At 1330 hrs, A, B and C Coys were completely surrounded by the enemy. The majority of their automatic weapons had been knocked out by the previous bombardment and they had no amn. An attempt was made to withdraw the survivors of these coys under cover of smoke, but only a few got back to BnHQ at 908725. During the morning our losses had been heavy but a great many of the enemy had been accounted for. The enemy attacked with at least two coys on each of our coy posns, with a vast superiority of automatic weapons. Armd sp was requested by us, and was promised, but never reached our posn. BnHQ was under fire all morning. Lt-Col Meldrum was able to visit coy posns on foot during the early morning, but later went fwd in the FOOs tk, until this was subjected to direct enemy .88 mm fire. Evacuation of casualties was difficult and stretcher bearers moved all day under fire. Capt R. M. Caldwell, the unit MO, attended casualties under fire, in the fwd posns. As soon as the coys had withdrawn, arty was brought down on the town, but this did not dislodge the enemy who had now surrounded BnHQ area by fire. D Coy, alone, withdrew nearly intact to a def posn around BnHQ. Carriers patrolled the area and no enemy passed through the Bn posns to the rear. The remnants of the Bn held on until 2000 hrs when a barrage, by 4 regts arty, was laid down, starting from BnHQ and moving up to the South side of the rly. The 1 Scot R put in an attack on the village supported by the 6 Armd Regt, which restored the situation. The Bn was withdrawn at 2300 hrs to La Bergerie Farm. Maj F.E. Hodge, OC A Coy, Capt P.E. Gower, OC B Coy were missing. Three coys had been almost completely wiped out. The flank protection gp remained intact at Bronay.

Instructions regarding
preparation of War
Diaries; are contained in
F.S. Regs. Vol. 1.

WAR DIARY

Original, duplicate and
triplicate to be forward-
ed to O. i/c 2nd
Echelon for disposal.

Regina Rifle Regiment

June 7, 1944.	*During the night, the enemy pulled off a counter-attack on 'B', 'C' and 'D' Coys positions which was repulsed by our troops. The Bn was determined to stay put on the final objective.*
June 8, 1944. 0850 hrs.	*Weather - fine and clear.* *At 0850 'D' Coy reported that they were being mortared. At 0858 enemy tanks were seen at 963703. 8 enemy tanks were seen at 9770 and reported to Bde HQ. At 1220 enemy tanks were reported advancing along road to our HQ. at 1100 hrs, 'D' Coy reported enemy tanks in considerable strength 1000 yds to their front. 'D' Coy moved to 919713 to improve the Bn fortress. 'C' Coy report they had repulsed an infantry attack but were being attacked by tanks and requested arty support. This was granted. Attack was repulsed. The Bn still sits on objective. Bn HQ attacked by Panther tanks and infantry beginning at 2230 hrs.*
June 9, 1944 0030 hrs. 0423 hrs.	*At 0030 hrs Bn HQ was shelled and machine-gunned, when the enemy put in a tank and infantry attack on the town. One Panther tank pulled up outside Bn HQ. The tank was then knocked out by a PIAT. Meanwhile a hot time was had by all as enemy tanks were all about the town blasting away at the men in their slit trenches and destroying one of our A/Tk guns. The whole sky was lit up by blazing roofs and burning tanks as well as our own parachute flares. At 0220 hrs, another tank was knocked out by a PIAT near our mortar positions. At 0315 hrs, an enemy AA armd car SD KFZ 140 ran up the main street of Bretteville and was knocked out by PIAT fire in front of our Bn HQ. During the scrap, we lost seven carriers including one loaded with amn. In return five Panther tanks were bagged in the vicinity of Bn HQ. At 0423 Panther tanks left vicinity of Bn HQ and RVd a short distance away. We requested arty fire on them. This was granted. We were informed that tank support would be forthcoming at first light. At 0445 hrs, the enemy put in determined attacks on all Coys, but were thrown back. Altogether a very hectic night was spent by all. A bright new page was written in the records of this Bn. Everyone fought magnificently and although the picture looked black, there was no sign of wavering anywhere. In this attack, Capt. R. G. Shinnan lost his life.*

M10 by O. N. Fisher. (12543) The M10 mounted a 3 inch anti-tank gun on a Sherman chassis. It was fairly effective at ranged of less than 1000 yards but was lightly armoured.

Brigadier Foster.....

On the afternoon of June 8th the Royal Winnipeg Rifles were overrun chiefly owing to the fact that one assault company had been practically obliterated on the beach and the gaps in the ranks had to be replaced by reinforcements of all sorts, some not even infantry. There had been no time for reorganization.

The Regina Rifles were at Bretteville with one company at Norrey. Foster wanted that company to withdraw but Lt. Col. Matheson and the company commander protested vigorously that they would only have to capture it later. They were allowed to remain ...

The German attacks were launched without any tactical sense. The flanks of our battalion were exposed, a carefully concentrated flank attack might have been deadly, the enemy flung himself straight against the strongest points and utterly failed to exploit the undoubted weakness of his opponent's position.

The outstanding feature of the assault was the admirable spirit of the men and the excellent support fire of the artillery. No request for support fire went unanswered and many infantry understood, for the first time, that the gunner's role was something other than to block traffic.

Men of 'D' Company, Regina Rifles 8-10 June. PA 129042/ Public Archives Canada.

Patrol in Bretteville-L'Orqueilleuse by W.A. Ogilvie, (13499).

Instructions regarding preparation of War Diaries; are contained in F.S. Regs. Vol. 1.	*WAR DIARY*	Original, duplicate and triplicate to be forward- ed to O. i/c 2nd Echelon for disposal.

Canadian Scottish Regiment

June 8, 1944.

The attack went in at 2030 hours supported by a small artillery barrage and close support by tanks and was of a frontal nature ... Enemy opposition consisting of all types of MG, Mortar and Shell-fire was bitter almost from the Startline. The country was mainly flat wheatfields with orchards giving excellent concealment for the enemy. The men advanced without a falter into a veritable wall of fire, their courage was magnificent. Evidence of their feelings are well portrayed in the words of Cpl. Bob Mayfield of 8 Platoon who turned grinning to his section as they swung into the advance, 'Boy, this is going to be one hell of a good scrap!' And this spirit was maintained throughout. The casualties were naturally heavy but never a wounded man whimpered - the opposite in fact was the case and time and again badly wounded men had to be ordered back ... . As the objective was neared A company more or less merged with D who had been slowed by the enemy defense and, in addition, had lost their company commander, wounded 2 i/c and CSM killed ... . With magnificent coolness Major Plows walked about organizing the two companies ... . It was questionable whether the men were more human or devil at this stage, the latter conviction being borne out by the action of men like Cpls. Dodd and Jebes and Pte. Mulcahy who took turns jumping to the top of the bridge with a Bren gun at the hip and spraying the enemy, laughing gleefully as they did so.

Troops of the 3rd Anti-Tank Regiment, Royal Canadian Artillery move a 17 pounder into position June 10th. PA 128793/Public Archives Canada.

Allied Strategy

By the evening of June 9th the Allies had linked up their four eastern beachheads and were confidently moving to close the gap between the 'Utah' and 'Omaha' areas. Montgomery, acknowledging the extent of German resistance in front of Caen now proposed a pincer movement around the city with the 1st British Airborne dropping behind Caen to complete the encirclement. This scheme was far too ambitious and intense German attacks on the bridgehead over the Orne to the east of the city foreshadowed the failure of the left wing of the pincer. The assault on the right wing involved an attack by the 7th Armoured Division 'The Desert Rats' which was to wheel around the German positions and capture Villers Bocage, astride an important road junction. The 50th Division, holding the line to the west of the Canadians was to support the 'Desert Rats' by an advance of its own and the Canadians in turn were told to prepare a limited striking force to assist the 50th's attack. Nothing went according to plan.

The British armour ran smack into the German armour reserves and was withdrawn from Villers Bocage after a one-sided encounter with Tiger tanks. The 50th Division took very heavy casualties and made no progress. The Canadian thrust, directed at Le Mensil Patry, was a disaster.

The Queen's Own Rifles and the First Hussars were to lead off this attack from Norrey-en-Bessin on June 12th but early on the morning of the 11th word was received that the assault was to go in that afternoon. There was no artillery support and no time for reconnaissance. Brigadier Wyman of the 2nd Armoured Brigade, who planned the attack, was breaking every rule of Allied battle doctrine, but then so was everyone in the hastily improved battles of this period. Montgomery, and Dempsey, his Army commander had not yet accepted the fact that the Germans would defend Caen with all their resources. Dempsey had been ordered to 'proceed relentlessly with the original plan' and he did so, pressing on without the careful preparation of set piece attacks which was to characterize the rest of the campaign in Normandy.

The Canadians with 114 fatal casualties in their 'charge of the Light Brigade' to Le Mensil Patry, were no harder hit than the British forces on their flanks. The 51st Division's 5th Black Watch Regiment lost practically an entire company 'in point of fact every man in the leading platoon died with his face to the foe' at Breville and the divisional history is merciless in its condemnation of the 'hastily arranged' attacks. The 50th Division and the 7th Armoured had also suffered severe losses.

The battles of June 10 to 14th marked the end of the first stage of the Anglo-Canadian assault on Caen. Montgomery wanted time to build up his forces and he ordered General Crocker's First Corps, including the Canadians, 'to be on the defensive . . . . but aggressively so'. The Americans were to push hard for Cherbourg while a new plan for encircling Caen was developed. Montgomery did not, in fact, renew the attack on Caen until June 26th, the day on which Cherbourg fell. This delay was partly due to the great storm of June 19-20, but it is also clear that Montgomery was plagued by indecision, torn between his desire to apply overwhelming force to the battlefield and the fear that German reinforcements would tilt the balance in their direction.

'Epsom', the June 26th British operation on the right flank of the Canadian position, required the support of our divisional artillery, but it was not until July 4th that the Canadians launched a new attack of their own. For the 3rd Division the three-week pause was an opportunity to rebuild their shattered assault regiments and gradually condition the reinforcements to life on the front line. There was plenty of opportunity to learn. All battallions were required to send out nightly patrols to probe at the German lines and try to take prisoners. Most nights the Luftwaffe, chased from the daylight skies, would visit the bridgehead and the noise of its bombs was drowned out by the chorus of anti-aircraft guns. Movement during the day, particularily of vehicles, brought instant shelling and mortaring so life revolved around the slit trenches which often became quite elaborate 'homes'.

During the last week of June everyone was on edge waiting for their part in 'Epsom'. The Canadians were to move into Carpiquet and the Buron-Authie killing ground once the British offensive had reached its objectives. Code named 'Ottawa', this plan was cancelled on the 29th when it was clear that both 'Epsom' and a limited push by 3rd British Division on the Chateau de la Londe had failed. One battalion of the 3rd British Division suffered 161 casualties in that attack, an indication of just what the Canadians would face when their turn came.

With the benefit of hindsight, historians have usually seen the agony of the bridgehead battles as the necessary prelude to the near encirclement of the German armies at Falaise. For the soldiers of both sides who fought in front of Caen the battles were matters of life and death, not a prelude to anything. The German positions around the city were immensely powerful. Strong points were lightly held but the approaches were covered by machine gun, mortar and artillery fire, all of it carefully plotted so that any one area could be deluged on demand. German battle doctrine called for instant reaction to an Allied advance. The start line of the Allied attack, the area immediately behind the opening artillery barrage, was bombarded and as the barrage moved forward, the German artillery followed it. If a German position was overrun it was instantly subjected to heavy fire, even if German soldiers were still fighting - then a counter-attack would be put in.

The German army had learned the techniques of defence in depth on the Russian front and Normandy provided a better terrain for putting the lessons into practice. Historians have been very critical of the effectiveness of Allied infantry in the Normandy battles. Echoing the more arrogant German commentators who claimed that the Allied infantrymen sufffered from low morale and total dependence on air and artillery support, too many historians have failed to appreciate the difficulties facing the attacker in Normandy. When the Germans attempted offensive operations, they came up against the same overwhelming firepower that they had used to decimate Allied units. From June 6th, when anti-tank guns of the 3rd British Division had stopped 21 Panzer Division through the attacks on Bretteville-Putot to the famous Mortain counter-offensive, the Germans suffered their heaviest losses when they abandoned their defences and moved out to attack.

Operations "Room" 7th Brigade, 14 June. PA 129041/Public Archives Canada.

General Montgomery had foreseen a bitter struggle in the bridgehead but had not imagined that German resistance would be so strong. With the Americans facing the 'jungle-like' bocage country which impeded all movement, the pressure on British Second Army to break through in the more open terrain at Caen was mounting daily. Eisenhower, his deputy Air-Marshall Tedder, and many others were growing increasingly critical of Monty's failure to deliver a large scale attack on the left flank.

Montgomery's severest critics were RAF officers who felt that the army was ignoring its mandate to secure the territory around Caen which was vital for the construction of advanced airfields. The airmen believed that their Spitfire and Typhoon squadrons were capable of altering the balance of power on the battlefield but not if they had to be based in England. Canadian Spitfires of 144 Wing were the first elements of 2nd Tactical Airforce to operate from a base in Normandy, beginning on June 10th; most squadrons could not make the move to France until much later. The more severe expressions of the Air Marshall's frustrations, such as Tedder's dismissal of Montgomery's Caen battles as 'company exercises', were no doubt unfair but their impatience was understandable. By late June, Dempsey's 2nd Army had fifteen divisions and seven independent brigades ashore, yet Montgomery was unwilling to press a major attack. He was not at all confident that any kind of victory could be achieved in view of the heavy commitment of German Panzer Divisions to the British sector of the front.

Montgomery's assessment of the situation was influenced by 'Epsom' the gruelling, bloody battle for the Odon river. In its planning stage 'Epsom' had been a big battle to be launched by the newly arrived divisions of British 8th Corps, supported on the flanks by units of both other British Corps. After two days of fighting a narrow salient had been won, but around it all the German Panzer Divisions in Normandy were gathered. The British went over to the defensive, holding their positions against repeated counter-attacks. Montgomery drew what was indisputably the correct conclusion from these events. If the British and Canadians could continue to hold the bulk of the German armoured divisions on their front through a series of limited attacks, they could wear down the Germans and create the conditions for an American breakout on the right.

This is what Montgomery proposed in his Directive of June 30th and, if he and his admirers had let the record speak for itself, there would be little debate about his conduct of the first stages of the Normandy campaign. Instead, Montgomery insisted that this Directive was a consistent part of a master plan that he had devised long before the invasion. Curiously, this view does a great disservice to 'Monty', for any rigid planning of operations before the German response was known would have been bad generalship indeed!

The decision to engage the German armour on the left and breakout on the right was accepted by Eisenhower and Bradley. Eisenhower, nevertheless, continued to urge Montgomery to attack in greater strength noting on July 7th, 'we have not yet attempted a major full-dress attack on the left flank ...'. Coming on the eve of 'Operation Charnwood', the frontal attack on Caen, this letter was not well-received by Montgomery. It was, however, justified for while Bradley's Army was engaged in a mass battle to fight through to St. Lo, Montgomery's plan for Caen involved just three divisions, followed by a smaller attack in the Odon bridgehead.

Fortunately, the Germans remained convinced that the major Allied effort would have to come on the British front. They believed their infantry divisions could successfully defend the Bocage country in front of the Americans and they concentrated their energies on building a defense in depth in the Caen sector. Ultra continued to provide the Allies with detailed information on German dispositions, so that the battle could be planned with full knowledge of the enemy's intentions.

A member of the French Resistance meets a Canadian soldier.
PA 129045/Public Archives Canada

Mobile Bath by George Douglas Pepper, (13731).

Private L.R. Decastye, Highland Light Infantry in his foxhole, 20 June. PA 129039/Public Archives Canada.

German Strategy

On June 17th, Hitler met with his senior commanders at Margival, a Fuehrer Headquarters established in 1940, from which he had proposed to direct the invasion of England. By that time the Allies had united their five beachheads and pushed forward to a line running roughly from just north of Caen to Caumont, to just north of St. Lo and were advancing across the Cotentin peninsula through St. Saveur de Vicomte. Most of that line was still within range of the large naval guns and completely dominated by the Allied airforce. Allied reinforcements kept pouring over the beaches on a regular schedule while the Germans reacted to Allied pressure by forcing worn-down divisions to hold their positions. When that became obviously impossible, they scrambled for reinforcements which had to travel considerable distances over a badly damaged railway network and constant air attack. By the middle of the month the Germans were bringing divisions from Holland and southern France. On June 11th, the 2nd SS Panzer Corps with two divisions (the 9th and 10th SS Panzer Divisions) was ordered to France from Lemberg, Poland but it could not possibly arrive before the end of the month.

During all this time, the German higher commands greatly overestimated the number of divisions available to the Allies in England. They continued to believe that the main invasion was still to come and that it would come somewhere along the Channel coast. Although many would begin to have doubts about such a second invasion, the weekly situation reports of Army Group 'B' emphasize this aspect of the strategic problem. Indeed as pressure on the Caen sector mounted, these weekly reports suggest the main invasion was to be carried out in conjunction with a break-through in this area. Not until the middle of July did it appear probable to Army Group 'B' that the Allied Command was more likely to use its reserves to strengthen the existing beachhead rather than to open a new one.

The discussions at Margival did not get very far. There was little time and although it was clear that the defensive fighting was quickly destroying the offensive capability of the armoured divisions, the only infantry divisions which could relieve them, were in the 15th Army. No one seems to have pressed for their release. Hitler on his part expressed great confidence in the effects of the 'VI' weapons, which had just begun to fall on London and were now being dispatched in ever greater numbers. All attempts to find military targets for them, such as beaches, or the English embarkation ports, were turned down. One VI appears to have gone off course and crashed near the bunker, causing an uncomfortable air raid alarm during the conference. Hitler left France almost immediately, leaving Rommel with a few days of renewed optimism and Rundstedt silent as usual. There was no basic change in German strategy nor any substantial increase in supplies and reinforcements. The Luftwaffe remained virtually absent from the battlefield - with serious results for supplies and morale. As the German soldiers expressed it 'If it's white, it is American; if it's black, it is British and if you cannot see it, it is the Luftwaffe!'

Yet the situation could only deteriorate further without some alteration in German policy. By the following morning it was clear that the US 7th Corps had succeeded in reaching the west coast of the Cotentin peninsula near Carteret, thus isolating Cherbourg. Only small groups of German infantry fought their way south. The local German commands were once again caught with contradictory orders which dissipated their forces and failed either to defend Cherbourg with cohesive units or bring them south in a coordinated movement while the US forces in their path were still relatively weak.

On June 22nd as though to mark the 4th anniversary of the German invasion, the Russian Army began its summer offensive against Army Group Centre. Within a few days the extraordinary magnitude of this offensive was felt and the whole of the German centre in Russia threatened to collapse. No more reinforcements for Normandy could possibly come from the Russian front.

On June 26th scarcely a week after the cutting of the Cotentin peninsula, the fortress of Cherbourg surrendered. Although it would take the Allies longer than expected to make this port operational, this event had two major consequences. In the long run it offset the possible advantages which the Germans might have expected from the great

90

A German tank races for cover. CFPU PL 31487.

An RCAF Typhoon. CFPU PL 31847.

91

storm which raged June 19th - 22nd seriously disrupting the Allied supply system, and it should have made it clear to the German Command that there was no longer any strategic reason for launching attacks which were designed to reach the beaches - they could not now hope to destroy the bridgehead. They could perhaps contain it or they could try to defeat the Allies in some battle outside the range of the naval artillery - the one element in their inferiority of fire power which they could neutralize by the simple expedient of moving a little further inland. But this last policy meant giving ground, a policy abhorrent to Hitler.

On June 28th Hitler summoned his senior commanders to Berghof for a second conference, to be held the same day. By that time many of the Generals had come to the conclusion that just holding the line in Normandy was not a rational policy because sooner or later the Allies would break through and there were no defensive positions or reserves to hold them anywhere. Geyr von Schweppenburg, in a long memorandum, argued that it was hopeless to try and attack within range of the naval artillery and he advocated, as he had all along, a more mobile defence. Rommel and Rundstedt passed the memorandum on to OKW with approving comments. Rundstedt also demanded greater flexibility and the creation of rearward defensive positions.

But the conference changed no one's mind and the hold-fast-at-all-costs policy was reiterated by Hitler. He understood that his generals no longer had any faith in either his or OKW's manner of defending Normandy, perhaps not even in his miracle weapons or the return of the Luftwaffe with jet aircraft which had been promised for some time. His response was predictable. Within days he relieved Geyr von Schweppenburg as commander of Panzer Group West and replaced him with General Eberbach, renaming the group 5th Panzer Army. On July 2nd he replace Rundstedt with Field Marshall Kluge, in the hope that this Field Marshall would bring a new wave of firmness and optimism to the western command. General Marcks had been killed on June 12 and Dollman, of the 7th Army, had died of a heart attack on June 29th. Only Rommel remained, despite bitter 'observations on the situation' which he wrote to Kluge after their first stormy meeting on July 3rd and which

were also read at Fuehrer Headquarters.

In fact these changes altered nothing. The campaign had already taken an unusually high toll of senior German generals in battle and the newer ones could do little more than respond to the immediate situation by feeding meagre reserves into threatened areas. If Hitler hoped that the arrival of the 2nd SS Panzer Corps in the last days of June would give the German armies some offensive power, he was badly mistaken. Their attacks on the right flank of the British salient along the Cheux-Buron axis on June 29th were delayed by air attacks and enormous concentrations of heavy naval and army artillery. (Ultra had again warned of the timing and direction of the attack.) They were barely able to prevent the British from enlarging their bridgehead across the Odon river. The 2nd SS Panzer Corps had arrived, as had all the armoured divisions, just in time to prevent the Allies from making a decisive break through, but too late to effect even a local counter-attack of any serious consequence.

The lack of infantry reserves had made it impossible to relieve those armoured divisions which had been on the front line since the first days of the invasion. Although some infantry now started to arrive from southern France (272nd, 276th and 277th Infantry Divisions), they would find it difficult to take over the assigned sectors because, as one of their commanders complained, the armoured divisions had fought a loose defence and had built few field fortifications. The lines could not be properly stabilized and the armoured divisions were continuously called back to 'fire-fight' individual Allied attacks.

Moreover, even when they were out of the line, the divisions received virtually no replacements. Almost no tracked vehicles reached the front, and the manpower situation remained critical. The practice of building new divisions rather than properly reinforcing existing ones placed an enormous burden on units that continued to be used as divisions when they were often hardly stronger than regiments.

Therefore, at the end of June, the German line held largely because individual units, particularly the armoured divisions, fought tenaciously and skillfully. Nearly all of them were either new or pulled out of the Russian front after being 'burnt out', as the German Command put it. Some had only a short period of training as units and few had recieved their full complement of weapons. Some had the numbers of old divisions as, for instance, the 21st Panzer Division. That division had, of course, been lost in Africa but Hitler insisted that it be re-established, as he had with nearly all the divisions lost in Africa or Stalingrad.

So the 21st Panzer Division was reconstituted in 1943 out of a few hundred men who had been home on leave or in rearward areas in Italy, some experienced officers from other units, and new draftees. But the armour was late in arriving and so, at the time of the invasion, much of the equipment was made up of captured French and Czech tanks, re-equipped with German guns in the workshops of the Division. The energy and efficiency of the commanding officer had much to do with its viability in battle.

However, a large proportion of the armoured divisions were units of the Waffen-SS and these were generally better equipped and had greater manpower than their Wehrmacht counterparts. Allied troops who had to face these divisions, found them formidable opponents. Since the Allied advance around Caen was slow and methodical and failed to exploit the opportunities which the slow reinforcement rate of the German line seemed to offer, some Allied divisions found themselves opposite the same German division for long periods of time. Nowhere was this more evident than in the sector held by the 3rd Canadian Division which was engaged with the 12th SS Panzer Division, 'Hitler Jugend', for the whole month of June and part of July.

The name 'Hitler Youth' was not just a fanciful designation for an ordinary armoured division. It was created as a result of high level consultation, initiated by the leaders of the SS and the Reich's youth leader, Axmann. An undated Fuehrer order authorized the establishment on June 1st 1943, of a Panzer Grenadier Division composed of volunteers from the Hitler Youth Movement. These volunteers, born in 1926, were gathered from all over Germany, released if necessary from other units or the labour force, and selected on the basis of leadership exhibited in their years as members of the Hitler Youth Movement. There was even a height requirement of 170 cm for the infantry (168 cm if they showed outstanding promise). Many were taken from wherever they were, even if they did not volunteer.

In October 1943, the Division was officially transformed into a Panzer Division although nothing really changed in its establishment. A large number of officers were brought from the 'Adolf Hitler' Division which had fought in the campaigns of France, the Balkans and Russia. A smaller number came from other units of the Wehrmacht, often selected because they had some connection with the Hitler Youth Movement.

It was a young division; the commanding officer, Fritz Witt, was only 35 years old and the men - boys really - were largely between 16 and 18. They had lived all their conscious lives in Nazi Germany, been nurtured in its youth organization, specially picked for their aptitude and enthusiasm. They had been playing at being soldiers all their lives, the hallmark of totalitarian youth organizations. Their officers found parade square discipline unnecessary; the Hitler Youth were used to obedience, but they did need combat training, with live ammunition. Their enthusiasm knew no bounds. They were the elite warriors of National Socialist ideology.

It was an ideology full of paradoxes. The officers claimed with pride that they behaved as substitute parents to the boys. No one under 18 was issued cigarettes, only a double ration of candy. There were to be no relationships with prostitutes, or indeed women generally; three months pay was voluntarily donated to the poor and the victims of the bombing at home. The virtues of motherhood, responsibility, self sacrifice and comradeship were extolled, so obviously were the tenets of National Socialism, the inferiority and decadence of their enemy, the glory of conquest and the superiority of the master race. The majority of the officers had had much time to put these latter theories into practice during three years of fighting on the Russian front. It added up to a dangerous combination of self-righteousness, brutality, patriotic fervour, sophisticated battle training and simplistic ideology.

Kurt Meyer, at his trial for the murder of Canadian prisoners of war, testified that he had never ordered or advocated the execution of POW's, but he had told his young soldiers:

'There is nothing honourable about imprisonment. After the end of each war every prisoner should be in a position to prove that he fell into captivity guiltlessly. Experiences of 1941, 1942 and 1943 taught us that there is no imprisonment for us. There was not one prisoner in my troop between 1939 and 1943 .... I wish you, my boys, no imprisonment .... The last shot belongs to you'.

Even if one believes that nothing else was said, such an attitude could hardly fail to bring about an equal reluctance to take prisoners. Certainly many Canadian soldiers were shot after they had been taken prisoner, some within the confines of Meyer's headquarters.

The Canadian 3rd Division faced a brutal enemy and a formidable one. General Eberbach testifying for the defence at the Meyer trial, reported that both he and his predecessor, von Schweppenburg, regarded the 12th SS as the 'corset stay' of the German Army in Normandy. Its success rate against any Allied troops measured in tanks knocked out, prisoners taken, weapons captured, was approximately three times the success rate of the 21st Panzer Division and double that of Panzer Lehr. The Canadian casualty rate reflected the unfortunate fact that for so long they were confronted by this terrible killing machine. Their achievement in overcoming this monstrous force should not be forgotten.

Hitler Youth, Nuremberg 1937.

Hitler Youth, Normandy 1944.
PA 129130/Public Archives Canada.

War Diary Panzer Group West

29 June 2145 hrs	O.B. orders SS Gruppenfuehrer Bittrich, who is in command of 2 SS Panzer Corps, to continue the attack throughout the night, so long as the forces last out. O.B. sees in this attack the great opportunity. SS Gruppenfuehrer Bittrich reports that the line Gavrus - Grainville -Raury, which had been taken by 1900 hrs. by 2 SS Panzer Corps. had to be given up, as the enemy supported his counter-attack with the most intense artillery fire. 10 SS Panzer Division destroyed 11 tanks; 9 SS Panzer Division destroyed 27 tanks. Comd. 2 SS Panzer Corps stresses the fact that this intense artillery fire has a very strong effect on morale.
30 June	The attack is halted by midday by the most intense enemy artillery fire. 2 SS Panzer Corps organizes a defence line on the heights 112 (NE Esquary) - Gavrus-Tessel Bretteville. In a telephone conversation between Comd. Seventh Army and C. of S. Panzer Gp, latter gives appreciation of the situation, especially drawing attention to the heavy fire of British naval artillery in the area of penetration, in which the attack of the 2 SS Panzer Corps also petered out.
1 July 1915 hrs	Telephone conversation C. of S. with S. of S. 1 SS Panzer Corps. C. of S. requests that a prompt report be made on casualties which the 9 and 10 SS Panzer Divs. suffered on both days of the attack, as well as a report on damage sustained from the air and from naval artillery. These data will be required for submission to the Fuehrer.
4 July 0715 hrs	Enemy goes into attack with infantry and tanks both sides of the Bayeux-Caen road. The first attack is repulsed. But the enemy has penetrated into Carpiquet with tanks. No report of success has come in, up to 1100 hrs, from 1 SS Panzer Corps. The enemy responds to our own heavy bombardment in the night of 4 July on Baron and the rest of the localities within the area of penetration with most intense artillery fire so that our own shock troops are unable to determine any successes whatsoever.
6 July 1000 hrs	C. of S. 1 SS Panzer Corps reports enemy reinforcements in Carpiquet and urges the evacuation of Caen, as in the event of an attack, the population would certainly render assistance to the enemy. He further requests the despatch of the Engineer Commander to 12 SS Panzer Div for the reconnaissance of two fords across the Orne for the passage of 12 SS Pz Regt.
8 July 2100 hrs	Marshal Rommel arrives for a consultation with the O.B. at the command post of the Pz. Gp. Marshal Rommel gives his approval to the withdrawal of the heavy weapons from Caen and regrouping in depth.

Pz. Gp. thereupon orders 86 Corps and 1 and 2 SS Pz Corps to withdraw all heavy weapons from Caen that same night. Strong infantry forces, supported by engineers, remain behind and are to offer resistance on the line Calix - P64 north of Caen - northern outskirts of St. Germain - airdrome 300 m south of eastern extremity of Carpiquet. Only in the case of superior enemy strength is a withdrawal to be made to the line: east bank of the Orne - northern outskirs of Venoix and northern fringe of Bretteville. |

Burnt out Mark IV Tank and dead German soldier by W.A. Ogilvie, (13258).

Carpiquet

If the overall plan relied on an American breakout, Dempsey's Second Army was still required to capture Caen and maintain constant pressure on the Germans. Accordingly, preparations for 'Charnwood', a three-divisional frontal assault on Caen, were begun with July 8th as the target date. It is not clear why General Crocker, who was to command 'Charnwood' ordered the 3rd Canadian Division to capture Carpiquet before the main attack since the assault would place the Canadians in a narrow salient onto which fire could be directed from three sides. 'Ottawa' had been an operation which was closely coordinated with 'Epsom' and the Chateau de la Londe battle but 'Windsor', the new plan for the capture of Carpiquet, was to be assisted only by a very limited move on Verson by a brigade of the British 43rd Division who were to 'temporarily occupy the village ... during the night before the attack' and a diversionary move on Gruchy by the Sherbrooke Fusiliers.

The 8th brigade, strengthened by the addition of the Royal Winnipeg Rifles, was to make the attack with the support of twenty-one regiments of artillery, the tanks of the Fort Garry Horse, and three squadrons of Flails, Crocodiles and Petards from the 79th Armoured Division. Two squadrons of Typhoons were on call and HMS 'Rodney's' 16 inch guns would be used to soften up the target before the attack. All of this additional fire-power made for an impressive barrage, but it did not prevent the Germans, who had every square yard of the area plotted for artillery fire, from wrecking havoc with the infantry. The four battalions had to cross more than a mile of open country. When the Allied artillery opened up at 5:00 a.m. the Germans instantly shelled the infantry's start line and continued to rain down high explosives on the men who struggled forward through the wheat fields.

The North Shore Regimental History calls Carpiquet 'the graveyard of the regiment' because it sustained its heaviest casualties of the war on July 4th. But, the North Shores were a 'lucky' regiment compared to the Royal Winnipeg Rifles. The Winnipegs had suffered so many losses on D-Day and in Putot that their casualties on July 4th, which were almost as high as the North Shores, were just another horror to be endured.

Reading the War Diaries and after-battle narratives of the survivors of Carpiquet is a chilling experience. Major J. E. Anderson of the North Shores spoke for everyone when he wrote,

> *"I am sure that at some time during the attack every man felt he could not go on. Men were being killed or wounded on all sides and the advance seemed pointless as well as hopeless. I never realized until the attack at Carpiquet how far discipline, pride of unit, and above all, pride in oneself and family, can carry a man even when each step forward meant possible death."*

The men of the assault regiments did keep going forward. The North Shores and the Chaudieres occupied Carpiquet village and dug in. They were joined by the Queen's Own Rifles who were supposed to press on to the airport control buildings. But the Royal Winnipeg Rifles had been unable to capture their objective, the hangers on the south side of the runways. Here the Germans had waited in concrete pillboxes to add heavy machine gun fire to the torrent of mortar and artillery shells. A second attack with tanks and flame-throwing Crocodiles failed to dislodge the young SS troops and at 9:00 p.m. both the Queen's Own Rifles and Winnipeg attacks were called off.

For the troops in Carpiquet the fighting could not be called off. Exposed in their finger-like salient they were subjected to continuous fire from a German mortar brigade which had been attached to the 12th SS. Tank and infantry counter-attacks pressed to the very edge of the pile of rubble that had once been a village but the 8th Brigade held on until the main attack on Caen forced the Germans to withdraw.

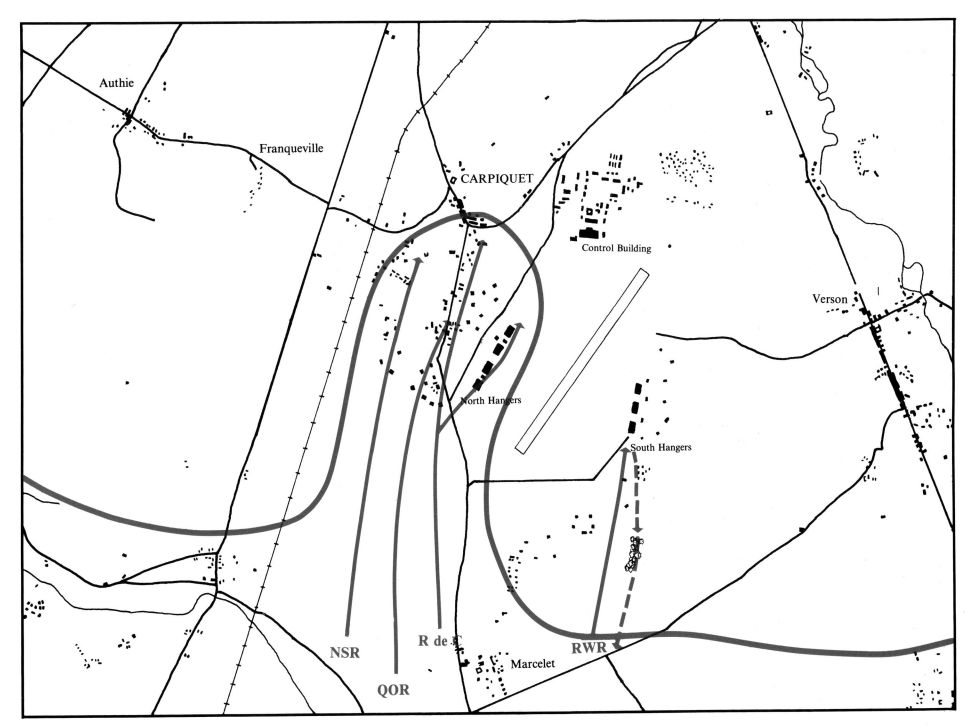

Authie

Franqueville

CARPIQUET

Control Building

Verson

North Hangers

South Hangers

NSR

QOR

R de C

RWR

Marcelet

Instructions regarding preparation of War Diaries; are contained in F.S Regs. Vol. 1.

WAR DIARY

Original, duplicate and triplicate to be forward- ed to O. i/c 2nd Echelon for disposal.

Royal Winnipeg Rifles

Marcelet July 4, 1944.

The Bn stood to 50% during the night and at 0500 hrs our arty preparation began. There was a barrage on Carpiquet village which bns of 8 Cdn Inf Bde assaulted and concentrations fired on the hangars on the airfd, our objective. The start line of the barrage was very close to our C Coy posn, and our own shells landed very close to them. The enemy began to mortar us at once, which seems to be their policy, to follow our own barrage with their fire. A and D Coys started their advance at 0530 hrs against the hangars in sq 9668, supported by B and C Coys. A and D Coys suffered heavy casualties from the time they crossed the startline, until they neared their objectives, from enemy mortar fire. Enemy MGs opened up from the hangars. A Coy reached their objective 100 yds east of the hangars but D Coy was held up by enemy wire obstacles and fire. B Coy was sent fwd to assist D Coy and by 0900 hrs the two coys had reached the first hangar. Two Sherman tks and four flame throwing Churchills (Crocodiles) were sent to get the enemy out of their pillboxes in the hangars. The tks suffered some losses and left and the the Crocodiles proved useless. D and B Coys withdrew to a copse west of the hangars. There were no tks in sp of our bn attack, and the arty preparation had not succeeded in knocking out the enemy pillboxes. The village of Carpiquet was taken with little resistance. The CO called the coy comds back to the start line at 1300 hrs. We were given a sqn of Shermans and after a further arty concentration on the hangars another attack was launched. The fwd coys again reached the first hangars, but the enemy's aimed arty and mortar fire from high ground on our right made it impossible for our now reduced coys to hold this ground overnight, as we were now being counter-attacked by enemy tks. At 2100 hrs Bde ordered the Bn back to the start line and the enemy posns and tks were attacked by our Typhoon aircraft. Rfn Knott and other drivers did excellent work during the day, evacuating our casualties in jeeps with stretcher frames fitted. All Coys patrolled their areas during the night, and the whole Bn area was shelled and mortared, causing further casualties to personnel and vehs.

Carpiquet Airfield by O.N
Fisher, (12439).

Instructions regarding
preparation of War
Diaries; are contained in
F.S Regs. Vol. 1.

WAR DIARY

Original, duplicate and
triplicate to be forward-
ed to O. i/c 2nd
Echelon for disposal.

Régiment de la Chaudière

July 4, 1200 hrs.	*The companies organize a solid defense on the south edge of Carpiquet village facing the enemy. Company 'C' is counter-attacked by German infantry and Panther tanks but repels the attack. The head-quarters of the battalion are established in a dugout constructed by the Germans. The dugout is very solid but attracts the almost constant fire of the enemy. All afternoon and night the Germans deluge our positions with artillery shells and mortar bombs. We lose a lot of men dead and wounded.*
July 5, 1944.	*We occupy the same defensive positions in Carpiquet. We attempt to establish a minefield in front of our position but the German fire is too intense and we are forced to wait until later to complete it. Carpiquet has become a true inferno. The German artillery and mortar submits us to an almost continual bombardment, but we are holding well despite the complete lack of sleep. The dugout serving as battalion headquarters receives three direct hits.*
July 6, 1944.	*Always at our same defense posts under the same mortar and artillery fire. Our losses in personnel mount. Counter-attack on 'C' Company repelled, Major Seveigny, the commander and his second-in-command, Capt. Rousseau, are wounded and have to be evacuated.*

Dive Bombing at Carpiquet by Paul Alexander Goranson. (11354).

Troops of the Cameron Highlanders of Ottawa firing Vickers machine gun near Carpiquet, 4 July. PA 129037/Public Archives Canada.

Canadian troops examining the bunkers which were the cornerstone of the German defence of Carpiquet airport.
PA 116513/Public Archives Canada

Caen

Carpiquet, like a number of other battles fought by British Second Army in June and July, illustrates a fundamental criticism that has been directed at Montgomery's conduct of the campaign in Normandy. Too often it is argued Second Army committed a brigade rather than a division, a division rather than a corps and a single corps when the whole resources of the Army should have been brought to bear on the enemy. One explanation for this policy, which brought sharp comments from Eisenhower's headquarters as well as from soldiers in the field, is that Montgomery would not attack without massive artillery support and the build-up of supplies in the bridgehead was much slower than expected. There was no easy answer to the problem confronting Montgomery and Dempsey in the bridgehead. The bitter complaints of battalion commanders who cursed limited attacks because they allowed the full weight of German artillery to be brought to bear on a small section of the front are hard to argue with, but no one wanted to attack without the largest possible measure of artillery support.

For 'Charnwood' the attack on Caen, Montgomery had decided to use the three divisions of 1st British Corps. A front of some eight miles would be struck, more or less simultaneously, on the morning of July 8th. To supplement the artillery and naval guns, arrangements had been made with Bomber Command to join in on the preliminaries. This was to be the first use of heavy bombers in direct support of the army and no one knew exactly how to obtain the best results, or what to expect. Fear of bombs hitting our own troops led to the selection of a 'bombline' three miles beyond our positions. The area chosen, a rectangle along the northwest edge of Caen, was well inside the ring of fortified positions held by the Germans. The vast armada of Lancasters arrived over the battlefield on the night of July 7th, six to eight hours before the infantry assault.

All reports agree that for the soldier in his slit trench the never-to-be forgotten sight of an endless stream of bombers blasting away at the enemy was an enormous boost to morale. It is equally clear that rear-echelon German troops received a tremendous shock and the dramatic demonstration of Allied power affected everyone among the enemy. Unfortunately, the bombing had virtually no impact on the capacity or the will to resist of the German troops in the defensive perimeter. The destruction of large parts of Caen and the death of many civilians must be added to the balance sheet as well.

The old problem of an open flank which had confounded the Canadians on June 7th was to be overcome by folding the front in from the left with the 3rd British and newly arrived 59th British Divisions starting off for Lebisey, Epron and St. Contest well before the Canadian 9th Brigade once more took the road to Buron.

The plan called for the Stormont Dundas and Glengarry Highlanders to capture Gruchy and the Chateau de St. Louis, while the Highland Light Infantry assaulted Buron. The North Novas would then be committed to take Authie and Franqueville. From this base the 7th Brigade would move off to Cussy, the Ardenne Abbey and, if all went well, Caen.

By H.Hour, 7:30 a.m., the 3rd British Division had captured Lebisey but the 59th British Division was still struggling to win its initial objectives, Galamanche and La Bijude. Once more Buron would be attacked with St. Contest in German hands. For the Highland Light Infantry, raised in Waterloo County, Ontario, this was to be their first major battle. The men of the battalion will never forget July 8th, 1944 or the ill-fated Norman village of Buron. The pattern was all too familiar; the troops moved off quickly and made it to the outskirts of the village with few casualties. The Germans had constructed a wide anti-tank ditch just north of Buron as their first line of resistance. When it was captured enemy artillery and mortar rained down on the position. The forward edge of the village was strongly held by a ring of defensive positions, most of which contained medium machine guns. Once the village was occupied a series of tank counter-attacks had to be beaten off; fortunately, an anti-tank battery of seventeen pounders had been attached to the regiment and its guns proved as fearsome as any German 88's.

The battle for Buron lasted all day but on the right flank the Stormont Dundas and Glengarry Highlanders captured Gruchy with much less difficulty. Aided by an unorthodox charge by the Bren gun carriers of the

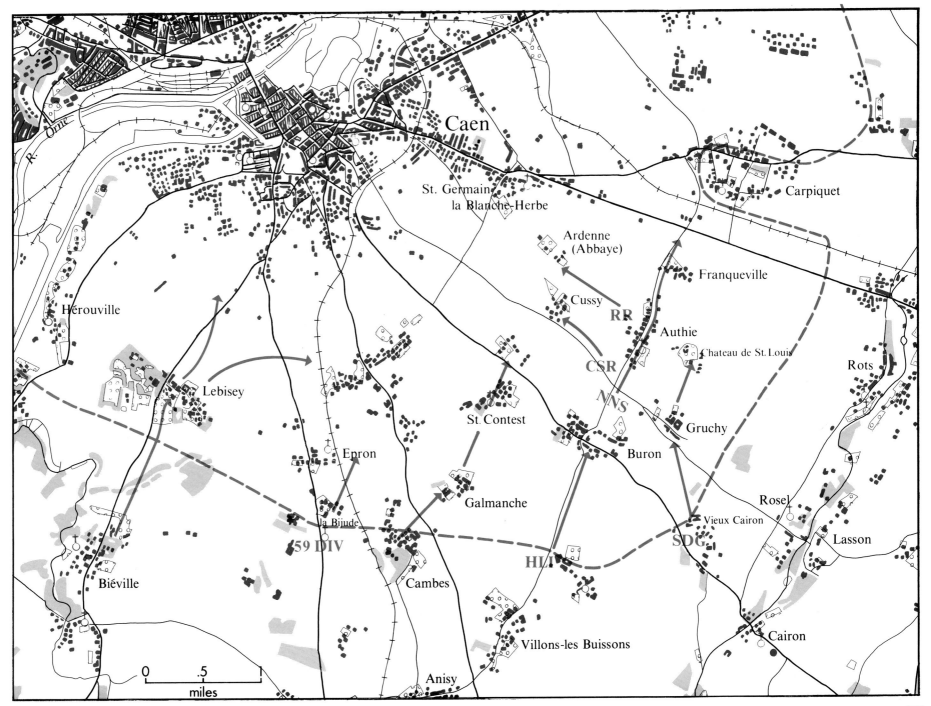

R. Orne

Caen

St. Germain la Blanche-Herbe

Ardenne (Abbaye)

Cussy

RR

Franqueville

Authie

Chateau de St. Louis

CSR

NNS

Rots

Hérouville

Lebisey

St. Contest

Gruchy

Buron

Epron

Galmanche

Rosel

la Bijude

59 DIV

Vieux Cairon

Lasson

SDG

HLI

Biéville

Cambes

Villons-les-Buissons

Cairon

Anisy

0   .5

miles

7th Reconnaissance Regiment, the Stormont Dundas and Glengarry Highlanders were able to report that they were ready to move on to the Chateau de St. Louis by 9:50. With Buron still in doubt this advance was delayed and the SDG's dug in, enduring heavy fire. The North Nova Scotia regiment had pushed forward to the edge of Buron, waiting for the order to attack Authie, but they too had to wait and 'very heavy casualties were inflicted ... by heavy mortar and 88 fire'. Despite continued shelling of Buron the North Novas passed through in the mid-afternoon and quickly seized Authie. The SDG's took the Chateau at about the same time and shortly thereafter the 59th British Division evicted the last German defender from St. Contest. Now it was the 7th Brigade's turn.

The Regina Rifles found that every movement towards the Abbey was checked by tank, mortar and machine gun fire. 'B' Company which made the first bound, suffered sixty-one casualties. 'C' Company which atempted to move through this base to the Abbey, were pinned down by a pillbox in one corner of the building and a light machine gun 'sniper' in the tower. By last light 'about twenty-one men all ranks' from this company were still in action. 'D' Company was able to make it to the walls of the Abbey 'under cover of 2 inch mortar and tank smoke'. Once there they dug in and waited for morning, protected by the wall of the fortress they were assaulting.

The Canadian Scottish found their approach to the start line contested by snipers and shell fire. Lt. Colonel Calbedu sought permission to stay well back until the attack was really on. 'I could visualize many casualties' he wrote, 'while waiting close to the start line for zero hour'. He assured Brigadier Cunningham that, 'we would make a forced march ... and hit it at the appointed ... hour'. At the appointed time, the Scottish were ready but so were the Germans. Both flanks were still held by the SS and the battle for Cussy became a long, confused action in which everything depended on individual courage and initiative. Towards darkness two companies of the Winnipegs were brought up to thicken the position before the anticipated counter-attack came in.

There was to be no counter-attack. However hard the day had been for the three divisions of 1st Corps, the German defensive ring around Caen had been broken. During the night Rommel had ordered the withdrawal of all heavy weapons south of the Orne and rearguards left in the battered city of Caen were in no mood to put up more than minor resistance on the 9th. Canadian and British troops were in the centre of Caen by mid-afternoon. The bridges across the river were down and the enemy firmly entrenched on the other side. But the city, which had loomed before the Anglo-Canadian forces since D-Day, was at last in their hands.

'Charnwood' had been a costly operation for everyone. The 3rd Canadian and 59th British Divisions had suffered more than a thousand casualties each. Exact German losses are unknown but the 16th German Luftwaffe Division was said to have 75% casualties and the sorely weakened 12th SS now contained about a quarter of the men who had so confidently arrived to fight the Canadians on June 7th.

Raid on Caen by Paul Alexander Goranson, (11433).

WAR DIARY

Highland Light Infantry

July 7, 1944.	*Morale - 100% as men are anxious to get at the enemy in Buron who have mortared and shelled us for over one month.*
July 8, 1944.	*The Bn was awakened at 0500 hrs by a terrific barrage laid down by the supporting arty along the whole Corps front. Members of the Bn assembled in Le Vey area were obliged to head for the slit trenches as the enemy opened up with a strong battery fire and dropped many into our area.*
	At 0730 hrs the two assaulting coys crossed the start line and travelled down their axis of advance towards the objective.
	Little opposition was met on the ground until the A/tk ditch was struck but both coys come under MG fire from the ditch. The ditch and auxilliary defensive positions behind it were cleared after some heavy close in fighting and many enemy were killed and about 20 PWs were taken.
	From the A/Tk ditch, which cut both the Les Buisson-Buron and the Vieux Cairon-Buron roads and was 12 ft wide and 15 ft deep, to the edge of the village the two coys come under a hail of MG fire and ran into the enemy DF arty and mortar fire called down as soon as the ditch was overrun. Many casualties were suffered by our tps on the way in.
	The forward edge of the village was strongly held by a ring of defensive positions most of which contained MMGs. These brought down continuous and devastating fire on our tps and it was almost impossible to advance through. Many times our tps were pinned to the ground by it only to get up and go on as soon as it let up. The tks had to be called fwd on several occasions to aid the inf fwd.
	'D' Coy under Major J. H. Anderson was the first coy into the village. The tks were not able to follow them in as they struck a minefield on the rt flank, 'D' Coy had to smash its way through alone and clean out all the trenches that comprised the defensive system. They suffered hy cas doing this and progressed on to the orchard on the right fwd side of the village with only half a coy.
	In the orchard Sgt. Herchenratter reorganized the remnants of two platoons and led the attack at clearing out the orchard. Cpl. Weitzel already wounded here distinguished himself by leading two men left of his section into an attack on two well sited MG posts. When both of them were hit he continued on and knocked out both posts before he himself was killed.

Instructions regarding preparation of War Diaries; are contained in F.S. Regs. Vol. 1.

WAR DIARY

Original, duplicate and triplicate to forwarded to O. i/c 2nd Echelon for disposal.

Highland Light Infantry

July 8, 1944.

Meanwhile, 'B' Coy was encountering heavy opposition on the left flank. They charged again and again but were faced with a strong reinforced coy equipped with at least double the usual number of automatic weapons. Tks were called for but were out of communication. When contact was finally made the tks feared to move fwd because of the minefields. It was sometime before they could be told that the left flank was free.

With the support of the tks 'B' Coy was able to break their way through the defensive ring and proceed to clean up the enemy MG posts one by one. These posts were very well dug in and it was necessary to approach the pit to the very edge before the enemy guns in them could be silenced. Going was very sticky for a long time. In fact several isolated pockets offered up resistance until next morning.

While 'B' Coy was breaking through 'C' Coy who was follow up coy fought its way into the centre of the town between 'B' and 'D' Coy positions with only moderate opposition. It drove right down the centre and swung over to the left behind 'B' Coy taking up a position west of the Buron-Authie road.

'A' Coy, in reserve, followed 'C' Coy in and swung right in behind 'B' Coy. For the next few hours things were somewhat confused. Communications were disrupted due to cas among signallers and sets and no one knew what the situation was. The Comd Gp moved right up fwd behind the assaulting coys in order to keep control of the situation but could not contact the coys. The Carriers, A/Tks and Mortars moved up in behind the res coy.

At 1130 hrs the C.O. was able to get his Coy Comds in by means of runner and learned the state of affairs. 'D' Coy had only one officer (Major Anderson) and 38 O.Rs.; 'B' Coy had one officer (Mr. Chantler) and about 1/3 strength; 'C' Coy was about 50% strength and 'A' Coy about 66% of their strength. All had reached and taken their objective and were consolidating. Mortaring and shelling by the enemy from St. Contest and Bitot on the left flank were exacting a heavy toll by the minute. So continuous and severe was the shelling that even slit trenches were not safe. The enemy followed his old habits of bringing to bear all the fire he possessed on his own position once it was overrun.

To complete our defensive lay out 'C' Coy was ordered up to high ground to the south of Buron. 'A' Coy replaced 'D' Coy in the orchard as 'D' Coy was too weak to hold it against a counter-attack then forming up from the south-west of their position.

Instructions regarding
preparation of War
Diaries; are contained in
F.S. Regs. Vol. 1.

WAR DIARY

Original, duplicate and
triplicate to forwarded
to O. i/c 2nd Echelon
for disposal.

Highland Light Infantry

July 8, 1944.

During the afternoon the enemy continued to shell every corner of the village systematically and submitted many cas on our tps. There were too many cas for our stretcher bearers to handle and not enough Jeeps or stretchers available to handle all the cas. This was a very noticeable point and has since been corrected. Only a Jeep or Carrier could hope to run through the hy shell fire that cut the Buron-Vieux Cairon road.

'B' Coy was in for a shaky time when it was attacked by eight Tiger tanks. The counter-attack was repulsed and the tanks in support of that coy did noble work by knocking out six of the eight and driving the other two away at a cost of three S.P.s.

The Comd Gp, sheltered in an old German M.T. bay, was hit as orders were given to complete the last stage of consolidation on the high ground in front. This direct hit killed three signallers and Lieut. C. W. Sparks and wounded the Col and Major Hodgins and Major Durward and four ORs. By this time Major Anderson, Lieut. Chantler and Lieut. Campbell were the only officers left except for Sp. Coy officers. Most of the senior N.C.O.s had become cas and the Bn was about 50% strength.

The LOBs (left out of battle) were sent for and the Bn was reorganized. They dug in completely to hold what they had taken and endeavoured to get the rest of their cas out.

Night fell on a quiet, smoking village which had witnessed one of the fiercest battles ever fought in the history of war. It was the HLIs first big fight and the 8 July will go down in its memoirs as a day to be remembered. The ranks were sadly depleted and reorganization showed them to be thin on the ground - too thin to stave off a counter-attack in the night. Yet they doggedly dug in, determined that their days' work would not be in vain and though dead tired ready to go on to Caen the next day if the opportunity presented itself. One hundred percent stand-to was maintained during the night but the enemy had expended all his energy during the day and with the exception of a few snipers trapped behind the lines all was quiet and the night passed without event.

Stormont Dundas and Glengarry Highlanders by O.N. Fisher, (12618).

General Montgomery in Caen.
PA 129129/Public Archives Canada.

Regina Rifle Regiment

July 8, 1944.	*Operation 'Charnwood'*

'B' coy moved up to FUP at approx 1700 hrs from assembly area. In coming near Authie approx 500 yds away, 2 MGs opened up on us from front and from left flanks. The coy was in an open field and the leading section with the 2 IC got across a gap to bldgs near village. They continued to fire on the rest of the coy, and I, the 2IC, arrived at the start line with one section. The section suffered 2 cas on the way down. Remainder of coy with Maj E G Syme, Coy Comd arrived about 15 mins later. Considerable sniping with several MGs were still at large in Authie at this time. It was 30 mins before coy was formed up ready to move to objective, 10 and 12 pls forward with 11 pl following up. All reached objective under hy mortar fire about 30 mins later and consolidated there. We mopped up around objective. Mgs and mortar OP, and two tks were firing on us from Abbey and the coy took protection in strong point area. Total cas during the day was 61 all ranks.

'C' coy moved off from assembly area to start line approx 1725 hrs. As we were moving towards Authie into heavy mortar fire. We arrived there about 1815 hrs. We waited there for 'B' coy to move forward and formed up on the start line. After 30 mins in Authie, we moved along axis of advance towards first objective, which 'B' coy was clearing and consolidating on. We passed through 'B' coy and ran into very heavy mortar fire and fire from two tks. 'D' coy was also pinned down. One LMG was in pillbox at corner of Ancient Abbey and one LMG sniper was on top of the Abbey. Here 13 and 14 pls went right flanking, with 15 pl giving covering fire and moving up slowly. At this stage, heavy cas were suffered in all pls. Coy then withdrew to 'B' coy's posns on orders from Maj Tubb before he was wounded. Remainder of coy still in action amounted to about 21 men all ranks. About 15 of these crawled back to Authie on their own, the remainder staying in 'B' coy's posns. At Authie, the 15 men reported to Maj A S Gregory and were used as stretcher bearers.

'D' coy left assembly area about 1730 hrs, and were under shell fire all the way down, arriving at Authie about 1800 hrs. Cas suffered on the way down was one killed, one wounded and 1 jeep knocked out. Coy formed up on start line and received orders to move off about 1845 hrs. We proceeded along axis of advance to first objective and suffered one more cas from MG fire on the way to the first obj. Coy moved forward on axis passing through 'B' coy and moved forward with fire and movement to within 500 yds of the Abbey. We were then pinnned down with heavy MG fire from 2 tks at corner of Abbey, dug in pillboxes and MG on top of Abbey. 16 pl went left flanking, but were forced to withdraw under heavy MG fire. We then moved 17 and 18 pls in an assault on the Abbey under cover of 2 inch mortar and tk smoke about 2230 hrs and gained our objective.

The ruins of Caen.
PA 115526/Public Archives
Canada.

Retrospect

On July 5th the millionth Allied soldier landed in France. Operation 'Neptune' had been completed and the lodgement was secure, Cherbourg had been captured and that promised to ease the supply problem in the future by giving the Allies a major port. In the meanwhile the supply system functioned surprisingly well via the beaches and the one remaining artificial harbour. Caen finally succumbed after thirty-three days of bitter fighting but its fall did not open the way to an easy or rapid break-out.

The campaign had not gone quite according to plan but the Allies had accomplished a great deal. Above all they had managed to bring up their reinforcements more quickly than the Germans had been able to bring up theirs. By the beginning of July, Allied strength was in every respect superior, and their total mastery of the air and the sea gave them overwhelming fire power. They could be comfortable in the knowledge that German strength was insufficient to seriously challenge their position. It was unlikely also that the Germans could spring any surprises given the sophistication of the Allied intelligence system.

June had indeed been a frustrating month for the Germans. On both the Western and the Eastern fronts, their reserves had been stationed in the wrong places. They had expected the Russians to launch their offensive in the southern sector but the Russians had attacked in the center. They had expected the Allies to land on the Channel coast but the Allies had invaded in Normandy. The German High Command was reluctant to believe that it had made two such cardinal errors. Consequently it was slow to react, slow to release its reserves, allowing a dangerous situation to develop into catastrophe in July and August. On both fronts also, the Luftwaffe proved unequal to the task of defending the sky over the Army, making the movement of troops and ammunition very difficult.

Canadians had played a major role in all aspects of the 'Neptune' operation. On the sea, ships of the Royal Canadian Navy had fought in the only serious sortie made by German destroyers and had participated in virtually every phase of the naval operations. In the air, squadrons of the Royal Canadian Air Force were part of the huge fleet of aircraft which formed an almost impenetrable umbrella over the battlefield and inflicted such high losses on the German ground forces. On land, the Third Canadian Division, the Second Armoured Brigade and all their attached units had been in the forefront of the battle. They had been involved in some of the fiercest fighting because their position, immediately west of Caen, had been a pivotal one during the whole month.

Brilliant manoeuvres were rare in this part of the war, particularly on the part of divisional commanders. What counted was technical competence and determination and the Canadians demonstrated that they possessed both. It had not been an easy month for our soldiers. The landings, while not as difficult as that faced by the US troops at Omaha, had not been without problems and confusion. The advance inland had met, on the afternoon of June 7th, the most fanatical and best equipped German Division on the whole front and the fighting during the next five days had been particularly bitter. After the failure of the assault on le Mensil Patry, the Canadian part of the front remained relatively quiet until the attack on Carpiquet and the assault on Caen. Both were costly and neither was a complete success. Carpiquet was only partially captured and in Caen the bridges across the Orne river were not taken. General Crocker, the British Corps Commander, had hesitated just long enough to allow the Germans to evacuate most of their troops and equipment before the Canadian and British troops occupied the shattered remnants of the city. The Germans remained firmly entrenched in the suburbs on the other side of the river.

The Canadians had witnessed the first of the 'bombing carpets' laid down by Bomber Command the night before the assault on Caen. These would become a regular feature of future offensives designed to break out of the beach-head area. The 'bombing carpet' had probably made the initial assault easier but it had failed to make it easy enough to achieve a quick breakthrough. There was still no substitute for infantry and tanks fighting their way forward over ground disputed by the enemy.

The three offensive operations, including the actual landings, had cost the Third Canadian Division and its attached units, nearly 4,500 casualties, including 1,584 dead. Nor should it be assumed that the defensive fighting between June 12th and July 4th was without casualties; the local counter-attacks by the Germans were often sharp and resulted in bitter engagements. Exact figures are hard to obtain but both sides must have suffered seriously. On July 11th, the 12th SS Panzer Division was pulled out of the line to be replaced by the 272 Inf. Div. Its first staff officer, Major Hubert Meyer, estimated that the casualties of the Division from June 7th to July 9th had been about 4,000 dead and 8,000 wounded and missing, 60% of the original strength of the division. It had also lost about half of its tanks and self-propelled artillery. It was not quite like 1918, as many officers were beginning to say, but the human costs were nevertheless very high.

War is not about capturing territory; it is about imposing one's will on the enemy. The Allies were slowly but surely imposing their will on the German Army but for the soldiers, standing amidst the ruins of Caen looking towards Berlin, it seemed that they still had a very long way to go.

Maple Leaf Route, July 9th, 1944. PA 129035/Public Archives Canada.

INDEX

The Index is in two parts, part I lists the military units mentioned in the text: Part II lists the names and places. Page numbers indicated in brackets are for photographs: W.D. means War Diary: P.N., Personal Narrative etc.

Part I

Military Units and Headquarters

SHAEF: Supreme Headquarters of the Allied Exp. Force: 16, 17, 18, 26.

Canadian Units (Army)

Army 1st: 20.

Corps 2nd: 20.

Royal Canadian Artillery: 22, 98.
   Anti-tank Reg't 3rd: 74, (83).
   Field Reg't 12th: 68, 74.
   Field Reg't 13th: 74.
   Field Reg't 14th: 38, 60, 69.
   Field Reg't 19th: 38.

Royal Canadian Engineers: (34).
   Field Co. 6th: 48.

Royal Canadian Army Medical Corps: (76).
   Field Ambulance Unit 14th: 52.
   R.A.P. Staff: 52.

Divisions:

Armoured 5th: 20.

Infantry 1st: 20.

Infantry 3rd: 2, 20, 21, 22, 23, (24), 56, 64, 84, 93, 94, 108, 118, 119.

Brigades:

Armoured 1st: 21.

Armoured 2nd: 21,22, 53, (73), 84, 118.

Infantry 7th: 48-55, 56, 58, 64, 68, 69, 74, (85), 106, 108.

Infantry 8th: (35), 38-47, 56, 68, 98, 100.

Infantry 9th: 21, 56, 58, (59), 60, 64, 68-69, 74, 106.

Regiments:

Armoured:

1st Hussars (6th Armd.): 23, 48, 54, 58, 74, 84.

Fort Garry Horse (10th Armd.): 23, 38, 56, 98.

Sherbrooke Fusiliers (27th Armd.): 68, 69, 70, 71, 72, 98.

Infantry:

Cameron Highlanders of Ottawa (M.G.): 60, 68, 70, 74, 77, (104).

Canadian Scottish (CSR): 48, 51, (51), 58, 74, 77, W.D. 82, 108.

Highland Light Infantry of Canada (HLI): 68, (89), 106, W.D. 110-112.

North Nova Scotia Highlanders (NNS): 58, 68, 69, W.D. 70-72, 106, 108.

North Shore (New Brunswick) (NSR): 38, 42, (43) 56, 68, 98.

Queen's Own Rifles (QOR): 38, 40, W.D. 45, 58, 84, 98.

Regiment de la Chaudiere, (RdeC): 38,40, 45, 56, 58, 60, 68, 98, W.D. 102.

Regina Rifles (RR): 21, 48, P.N. 54, 58, 69, 74, W.D. 78, 80, 108, W.D. 115.

Royal Winnipeg Rifles (RWR): 48, W.D. 52, P.N. 53, 58, 69, 74, W.D. 77, 80, 98, W.D. 100, 108.

Stormont, Dundas & Glengarry Highlanders (SDG): 68,69, 72, 106, 108, 113.

Other:

Parachute Bat. 1st: 28, (29).

Recce. Reg't. 17th: Duke of York's Royal Canadian Hussars, 7th Recce. Reg't: 108.

British Units (Army)

Army 2nd: 20, 86, 98, 106.

Corps 1st: 20, 69, 84, 106, 108.

Royal Engineers: 27.

Divisions:

Airborne 1st: 84

Armoured 7th: 66, 84.

Infantry 3rd: 58, 64, 69, 85, 106.
   43rd: 98.
   50th: 2, 58, 64,66, 74, 85.
   51st: 66, 84.
   59th: 106, 108.

Regiments:

Black Watch (5th): 84.

Green Howards: 58, 74.

Other:

48th Royal Marine Commando: 38.

United States (Army)

Corps 7th: 90.

Divisions:

Airborne 82nd: 26.
   101st: 26.

Russian (Army)

Russian Army: 90, 118.

German (Army)

O.K.W. German Supreme Command: 8, 9, 10, 12, 16, 62, 64, 93, 118.

O.B. West German Command, West: 8, 9, 11, 12, 62, 66.

Army Groups B: 11, 62, 90.
   Centre: 90.
   G: 12.

Army Africa Corps: 11.
   1st: 12
   7th: 11, 62, 63, 64, 92, 96.
   15th: 62, 90.
   19th: 12.

Panzer Group West (5th Pz. Army): 12, 66, 92, W.D. 96.

Corps 1st S.S. Pz: 64, 96.
   IInd S.S. Pz: 90, 92, 96.
   IInd Parachute: 63, 66.
   LXXXIV Army: 62,63, 64.
   LXXXVI Army: 96.

Divisions (Armoured)

1st S.S. Leibstandarte Adolph Hitler: 12, 93.

2nd S.S. Das Reich: 12, 66.

2nd: 66

9th S.S. Hohenstaufen: 90, 96.

9th: 12.

10th S.S. Frundsberg: 90, 96.

11th: 12

12th S.S. Hitler Youth: 9, 12, 58, 62, 69, 74, 93-94, (95), 96, 98, 108, 119.

17th S.S. Pz. Grenadier, Goetz von Berlichen: 9, 12, 64, 66.

21st: 12, 58, 62, 63, 64, 85, 93,94.

Panzer Lehr: 12, 62, 64, 66, 94.

Divisions (Infantry)

77th: 64.

265th: 64.

266th: 64.

272nd: 92, 119.

276th: 92.

277th: 92.

346th: 64.

711th: 62, 64.

716th: 48.

Other:

3rd Parachute: 64.

91st Luftwaffe: 62.

16th Luftwaffe: 108.

Panzer Grenadier Divisions listed under Armoured.

Regiments:

12th S.S. Pz: 96.

25th S.S. Pz. Gren: 64, 69, 74.

26th S.S. Pz Gren: 64, 74.

192nd. Pz: 63.

736th: 56.

915th: 63.

Airforces

Allied (General):

2nd Tactical Airforce: 86.

Bomb-Carpet at Caen: 106, 118.

Canadian

R.C.A.F.: 118.

No. 6 Group: (16), 20.

No. 83 Group (Tactical): 20.

144th Wing (Spitfires): 86.

United States:

8th U.S. Airforce: 18.

German:

Luftwaffe - general: 10, 18, 84, 90, 118.

3rd German Air Force: 18.

K. G. 100 Squadron: 17.

Jet Aircraft: 92.

Navies

Canadian: 20, (31), 118.

Sioux, H.M.C.S.: (33).

British:
Home Fleet: 17.
Force J: 23, 32.
Hillary, H.M.S.: 56.
Rodney, H.M.S.: 98.
Submarines X20 and X23: 28.60.

German: 10, 17, 18.
E-Boats: 17.
U-Boats: 17.

Index Part II

A

Ainsy 64
Alanbrooke, Field Marshal the Viscount 10
Aldwinckle, Eric (war artist) -"Invasion Pattern" 36
Alexander, Gen. H. 14
Anderson, Maj. J.E. 98
Amiens 66
Anzio 12
Ardennes Abbey 64, (65), 69, 106, 108, 115
Arromanches 58
Atlantic Wall 2, (11), (13), 16, 26, 40, 64
Auckinleck, Gen. C. 10
Authie 64, 68, 69, 70, 71, 84, 106, 108, 111, 115
Axman, (Reich's Youth Leader) 93

B

B-25 18
Banville 48, 56
Barfleur 30
Benouville-Ranville Bridges 28, 63
Beny-sur-Mer 58, 69
Berghof 92
Berlin 119
Berniers 2,38, (44), 45, (46-47), 56,(59)
Bigot 22, (23)
Bitot 111
Blackader, Brig. K.G. (24), 58, P.N. 60

Bradley, Gen. O. (15), 86
Bray, Maj. 38
Bretteville l'orqueilleuse 69, 74, 78, 80, 85, 96
Breville 84
Brittany 64
Bronay 66, 74, 77
Buron 64, 68, 69, 70, 71, 72, 84, 92, 96, 106, 108,110, 111,112

C

Caen 28, 58, 63, 64, 69, 74, 84, 85, 86, 90, 93, 96, 98, 106-107, (116), (117), 118, 119
Calais 18
Calbedu, Lt. Col. 108
Calvodos 14
Cambes 69
Camilly 58
Caretan 63
Carpiquet 2, 56, 58, 64, 68, 69, 70, 84, 96, 98-105, 106, 118
Carteret 90
Caumont 66, 90
Charnwood 86, 98, 106, 108, 115
Chateau de la Londe 85, 98
Chateau de St Louis 106, 108
Chateau Vaux 51
Cherbourg 14, 66, 84, 90, 118
Cheux 74, 92
Chicosk, Rifleman 38
Churchill 14, (22)
Colombiers 58
Coningham, Air Marshall Sir Arthur (27)
Constances 63
COSSAC 14
Cotentin Peninsular 63, 90
Courseulles-sur-Mer 2, 48, (50), 54, (55), 56, 58
Crerar, Lt. Gen. H.D.G. 20, (21)
Crete 26
Crocker, Lt. Gen. J.T. 20, (24), 56, 69, 84, 98, 118
Croix-sur-Mer 48
Cunningham, Brig. D.G. 21, (24), 58, 68, 69, 108
Cussy 70, 106, 108

D

D-Day 19, 56, 58, 64, 69, 08, 108
Decastye, Private L.R. (89)

Dempsey, Gen. Sir Miles 84, 86, 98, 106
Dieppe 14, 56
Dietrich, Oberstzuppenfuehrer 'Sepp' 66
Divette River 28
Dollman, Gen. F. 63, 92
Doolittle, Lt. Gen. J. 16
Doubres 38
Duncan, Major 48
Dunkirk 30

E

Eberbach. Gen. H. 92, 94
El Alamein 16
Eisenhower, Gen. D.D. 14, (15), 16, 86, 106
Enigma Machine 17
Epron 106
Epsom 84, 85, 86, 96

F

Fabius III 23
Falaise 85
Feuchtinger, Gen. 62
Fisher, O.N. (war artist)
 -'The Atlantic Wall' 13
 -'The Rhino Ferry' 60, 'M-10' 79
 -'Carpiquet Airfield' 101
 -'Stormont, Dundas & Glengarry Highlanders' 113
Foster, Brig. H.W. (24), (51), 53, 74, P.N. 80
Franqueville 68,79, 106

G

Galamanche 106
Gavrus 96
Geyr von Schweppenburg, Gen. 12, 66, 92, 94
Gold Beach 2
Gooseberries 14
Goranson, P.A.
 -'Divebombing at Carpiquet' 103
 -'Raid on Caen' 109
Gower, Capt. 48
Grainville 96
Graye-sur-Mer 48, 52
Gruchy 106

H

Harris, Air Marshall Sir Arthur 16

Hayn, Major 62
Hebert, Lt. 38
Hillary, H.M.S. 56
Hitler, Adolph 2, 4, 6, (7), 8, 9, 11, 12, 16, 62, 66, 90, 92, 93
Hitler Youth (94), (95), see also under 12th S.S. Pz. Division

I

Isle of Wight 18
Ironside, Field Marshall, Lord 10

J

Juno Beach 2, 28

K

Keller, Maj. Gen. R. 20, (24), 56, 58, (60), 69
Kesselring, Field Marshall A. 11
Kluge, Field Marshal G. 92

L

La Bergerie Farm 77
La Bijude 106
La Delivrance 56
La Fresne-Camilly 58
Langrune 38, 56
La Vallette 48, 52
Law, Tony, (war artist)
 -'Canadian Tribal Destroyers Leaving on Patrol Plymouth' 31
Lebisey 106
Le Mans 18
Leigh Mallory, Sir Trafford (15)
Lemberg 90
Le Mensil-Patry 66, 84, 118
Les Buissons 58, 68, 69, 70, 71, 72, 110
Lessay 63
Le Mesnil 28
Le Vey 110
Lisieux 62, 64
London 90
Loire River 16, 64
Luc-sur-Mer 56

M

Madelaine 63
Marcks, Gen. E. 62, 63,92

Margival 90
Marshal, Gen. George C. 14
Matheson, Lt. Col. F.M. 54, 58, 80
Meldrum, Lt. Col J. 53
Merville Battery 26
Meyer, Lt. Col. 62
Meyer, Major H. 119
Meyer, Brigade Fuehrer K. 64, 69, 74, 94
Montgomery, Gen.B.L. 10, (15), 16, 20, (25),
    84, 86, 106, (114)
Morgan, Lt. Gen. F. 14
Mortain, 85
Mosquitoes 18
Mulberries 14
Munich 4
Munro,R, 56

N

Nan Green Beach 48, 55
Nan Red Beach 38, (38-39), 56
Nan White Beach 38
Neptune 14, 18, 20, 26-36, 118
Normandy 14, 16, 17, 20, 22, 28, 30, 62, 64,
    84, 85, 86, 90, 92, 94, 106, 118
Norrey-en-Bessin 69, 74, 80, 84
Nuremburg Rally (5)

O

Obersalzburg 62
Odon River 86, 92
Ogilvie, W.A. (war artist)
  -'Patrol in Bretteville' 81
  -'Burnt-out Mark IV and
     Dead German Soldier' 97
Omaha Beach 84, 118
Orleans 62
Orne River 26, 28, 62, 63, 64, 66,
    84, 96, 108, 118
Ottawa 85, 98
Overlord 14-19, 20, 22

P

Pas-de-Calais 14, 16, 17, 28
Patton, Gen. G. 16
Pepper, G.D. (war artist)
  -'Mobile Bath Unit' 88
Pointblank 20
Prague 4
Putot-en-Bessin 69, 74, 77, 85, 98

Q

Quebec Conferences 14
Queen Elizabeth (29)

R

Ramsay, Capt. 51
Ramsay, Admiral B. 14, (15)
Raneville 28, 63
Raury 96
Rennes 62
Resistance 62, (87)
Reviers 48, 54, 58
Rhineland 4
Robehomme 28
Rodney, H.M.S. 98
Rommel, Field Marshall Erwin (9), 10,
    11, 12, 62, 63, 64, 66, 90, 92, 108
Roosevelt, Franklin D. 14
Royal Military College 21
Rundstedt, Field Marshal Gerd von 11,
    12, 62, (63), 66, 90, 92

S

Salerno 17
Salmuth, Gen. H. 62
Schweppenburg, (see Geyr)
Seaburn, Capt. (34)
Sequeville-en-Bessin 58, 74
Seine River 16, 28, 64
Seulles River 2, 48, 52
Sicily 20, 56
Simonds, Lt. Gen. G.G. 20
Sioux, H.M.S. (33)
Smith, Gen. Walter Bedell 14, (15)
Speidel, Lt. Gen. H. 62, 64
Spitfires 86
Stalingrad, 93
Staubwasser, Col. 62
St. Aubin 2, 38, (40-41), (43), 56
St Contest 68, 70, 106, 108, 111
St. Croix-sur-Mer 51, 52, 58, 65
St. Germain 96
St. Lo 62, 86, 90
St. Mere Eglise 62, 63
St. Saveur de Viscomte 90
Sword Beach 26, 28

T

Tailleville 38, 56

Tanks: German strength 8-9
    D.D. Tanks 23, 27, 28, 38, 48
    Sherman 27, (73) A.V.R.E. 38, 48
Tedder, Air Marshal Sir Arthur 14,
    (15), 86
Tessier, Lance-Corp. 38
Thaon 58
Tierceville 58
Tilly-sur-Seulles 64, 66
Todd, Brig. P.A.S. (24)
Torch 14
Tours 66
Troarn 28
Trousers 23
Typhoons 18, 86, (91)

U

Ultra 17, 66, 86, 92
Utah Beach 26, 28, 84

V

V-Weapons 16, 90
Varville 28
Venoix 96
Ventriloquist 62
Verlaine 62
Versailles 2, 4
Verson 98
Vieux-Cairon Road 110, 112
Villers Bocage 66, 84
Villerville 30
Villons les Buissons 58, 70
    (see also Les Buissons)

W

Waterloo County, Ont. 106
Weimer Republic 2
Windsor 98
Witt, Brigade Feuhrer F. 93
Wood, Charles (war artist)
  -'D-Day'
Wyman, Brig. R.A. 21, (24), 84

Maps and Sketches

(All maps are reversed from normal
   (north) orientation.)

German Dispositions, June 6, 1944 10
The Overlord Plan 19

Operation Neptune

Typical Close Range Support 32
The Plan, Canadian Sector 37
The 8th Brigade Landinds 39
The 7th Brigade Landings 49
The Advance Inland D-Day 57
The Bridgehead: June 10, 1944 67
The 9th Brigade Advance 68
The Attack on the 7th Brigade 75
Carpiquet 99
Caen 107

SOURCES

This book is based on a new reading of the primary sources particularily the War Diaries of the Canadian units, Record Group 24 Public Archives of Canada; British, Canadian and German documents held by National Defense Historical Section, Ottawa and the microfilms of captured German documents, United States National Archives. Use has been made of the American, British and Canadian Official Histories as well as regimental histories. The authors will be happy to supply a full citation of any quotation or reference on application to the publisher.

ACKNOWLEDGEMENTS

This book could not have been produced without the co-operation and support of many people. The authors wish to especially thank: Barbara Wilson, Public Archives of Canada; W.A.B. Douglas, Director, and the staff of National Defense Historical Section; Mr. L. Azar, Canadian War Museum; K. Crouch and C.R. Watt, Library, Royal Military College; Brigadier D.G. Cunningham; Ross Munro; Arthur Stephen, James Hertel, Murray Corman, Wilfrid Laurier University; Jean Gourlay who typed the various drafts of the manuscript; the library staff at McGill University, Wilfrid Laurier University, University of Western Ontario, Fergus Public Library.

Terry Copp benefitted from a National Defense Fellowship which, among other things, permitted him to visit the Canadian battlefields in Northwest Europe. Our wives, Shirley Vogel and Linda Copp, listened, read commented and encouraged.